THE
ACTOR'S
FREEDOM

* * *

ALSO BY MICHAEL GOLDMAN

*   *   *

POETRY

First Poems

At the Edge

CRITICISM

Shakespeare and the Energies of Drama

THE
ACTOR'S
FREEDOM
TOWARD A THEORY OF DRAMA
* * *

Michael Goldman

The Viking Press * New York

LIBRARY OF CONGRESS CATALOGING IN PUBLICATION DATA
Goldman, Michael.
The actor's freedom.
Includes bibliographical references and index.
1. Theater. 2. Actors—Psychology. I. Title.
PN2039.G62   792′.015   75-1434
ISBN 0-670-10347-0

Printed in U.S.A.

Acknowledgment is made to Atheneum Publishers and Calder & Boyars Ltd. for material from The Persecution and Assassination of Jean-Paul Marat as Performed by the Inmates of the Asylum of Charenton under the Direction of the Marquis de Sade. *Copyright © 1965 by John Calder Ltd. Originally published in German. Copyright © 1964 by Suhrkamp Verlag, Frankfurt am Main. Reprinted by permission.*

For Rose Pollens Goldman
and Julius David Goldman

ACKNOWLEDGMENTS

$*\quad*\quad*$

I would like to thank Eric Bentley, Martin Meisel, and Daniel Seltzer, who have read this book in various drafts and given generously of their time and wisdom, both in seemingly inexhaustible supply. On classical matters, as on much else, I have benefited from the advice of Stephen Daitz and Kevin Whitfield.

I am also grateful to a number of organizations whose support has sped and sustained me in my work. The Elizabeth and Gardner Howard Foundation provided a grant under which this study was substantially begun, while a fellowship from the National Endowment in the Humanities allowed me a free year in which to complete it. Generous assistance also came from the Faculty Research Foundation of the City University of New York.

I am obligated, as so often in the past, to G. E. Bentley, this time for an invitation which allowed me to test out some ideas from the book in a lecture before the Shakespeare Association of America. A substantial portion of the third part, under the title "Identification: Towards a Theory of Drama," was given as the H. W. Reninger Lecture for 1973 at the University of Northern Iowa. My warmest thanks go to Daniel Cahill, both for his invitation and for the generous hospitality which made my visit so enjoyable. Some of my notions about ghosts were first broached in a lecture to the English Institute, for which opportunity it is a special pleasure to record my thanks to Walton Litz.

As ever, my deepest debt is to my wife Eleanor, who has suffered and discussed this book with me through all its drafts and stages. These formal sentences must stand for what they cannot express: the incalculable gift she has made me of her intelligence and love.

M. G.

New York
April 1974

NOTE

——————— * * * ———————

I use the word "theater" in these pages to refer not only to the place where plays are given but to the entire occasion of acted drama—that is, to the performance of parts by actors according to some kind of shaping intent. The notion is broadly inclusive, not limited to performances based on a written script, or even to the actor's taking on a character entirely separate from his own. It applies, that is, as much to the Open Theater's *Mutation Show* as to *Hamlet*. Most readers, I imagine, will find the definition natural enough, but I call attention to it because some interesting recent criticism has approached acting under the general heading of "performance theory," and defined "theater" to mean any occasion of performance. I use "theater" in the more restricted sense partly for convenience, of course, but I do insist on the difference between the theater of acting and other kinds of performance because I think it is a radical one. Acting *is* a type of performance, as speech is a type of communication, but in both cases the subclass is so distinctive, so rich and singular, that it can be misleading to treat it on terms of parity with other members of the general classification.

If anyone wishes to call a circus "theater," let him do so by all means. There are interesting points of similarity between circus and drama. And dramatic elements make their appearance in almost any kind of performance. But my use of "theater" does keep together under a single heading what centuries of artists all over the world have persisted in bringing together—what most people commonly have in mind when they say "theater." More important, it points to a distinction between this kind of theater and circuses, demonstrations, ballet, encounter groups, sports, religious ritual, etc., that corresponds to a widely held feeling—and the elaborate recognition of many cultures—that the theater of acting is very special, uniquely satisfying, like nothing else; that the difference is sharp, clear, and profoundly important; and that the theater of acting is as radically different from other kinds of performance as writing is from painting.

CONTENTS

* * *

PART I

* * *

ACTOR
AND
AUDIENCE

* * *

This book proposes a new way of thinking about drama. In my view, the forms of drama all flow from the confrontation that takes place between any actor and his audience; plays are best understood as ways of intensifying that confrontation and charging it with meaning. Drama, I shall argue, exists to satisfy a profound and largely unexplored human appetite, the appetite for acting—and to satisfy it means to make what goes on between actor and audience deeper, more sustained, more exciting and complete.

I start from what seem to me to be the elementary impulses out of which drama rises—the actor's impulse to act, and our answering desire to enjoy his art. I see the joint activity of actor and audience as a means by which man attempts to complete his relation to the world, especially to everything in the world that strikes him as dangerous and strange. My hope is to awaken the mind to the actuality of drama, what it is, why we are attracted by it, what it does with our lives. But I start with our experience of acting. To find out what plays are, what dramatic action is, what tragedy and comedy do, what happens in *Hamlet* (which is to say, what happens *to us* in *Hamlet*), why the *Marat/Sade* works, whether Aristotle was right—in short, to understand the nature of drama— it is necessary first of all to think about acting—about the nature of the actor's appeal, the kind of energy his art possesses, his relation to the audience and the world.

One aim of this study must be to develop a way of talking about drama that is not contaminated by notions derived from literature. The task is as difficult as it is essential, because drama, reduced to the words connected with it—scripts—looks very much *like* literature, often has a decided "literary" interest—and words are more at home talking about other words than about anything else. Hence literary criticism is at once the best developed and (relatively) the easiest criticism, and most criticism of the arts, especially of drama, tends to become literary criticism. This need not prevent it from being good criticism. One could, I imagine, pass a very profitable lifetime reading Shakespeare in entire ignorance of drama, as if his plays were nothing more than poems in dialogue form. One would not, in the end, have all of Shakespeare, or even most of him, but one might nevertheless have a lot. The problem becomes grave only when we begin to conceive of the aims of dramatic writing—to conceive, that is, of dramatic performance—in literary terms. Unfortunately, it is extremely hard to avoid doing so. In trying to think about drama, even in simply trying to enjoy a play, we constantly are influenced by expressions that seem to describe the processes of performance in a very natural and direct way—words like "imitation," "identification," "characterization"—but that are in fact thoroughly infused with misleading associations drawn from the experience of literature. For example, following

Aristotle, we describe what an actor does as *imitation*, which we tend to think of as a kind of representation. That is, when we use the word "imitation," we habitually speak as if the actor were a man bringing to our minds some object external to him (a "character") by manipulating media, which are in some sense also external to him. Now, this is what a writer does. But any moment of genuine exhilaration in the theater should remind us that it is not what an actor does.

The root power of the actor does not reside in his imitative ability. While any good actor is a good mimic, few good mimics are good actors. The impressionist stands lowest in the hierarchy of dramatic entertainers, the cliché notion of a deadly nightclub routine, yet most critical discussions of drama make no distinction between his skills and those of the actor. We all know better. An actor is not simply a man presenting a careful imitation of the behavior of other men, or even of his own behavior. His relation with what he imitates is never that of rough equivalency or representation. Acting is never simply mimetic; it appeals to us because of some other or more inclusive power. We feel an energy present in any good actor's performance that goes beyond the demonstration of what some "real person" is like.

One reason that the word "imitation" may cause trouble for us in thinking about the theater is that, whatever it is an actor does (and whatever name we choose to give it), it is very dangerous to equate it with what other artists do. Aristotle acknowledges that arts differ according to the media they use, but he never discusses the difference between the kind of imitation an actor carries out and that of the other arts; the difference between using one's body as a medium—one's entire body, that is, and all that animates the body—and using media distinguishable from one's entire body, like pigment or words or sound. He leaves the impression that the processes are essentially similar. The difference between them, however, is fundamental, and it leads to the defining qualities of drama.

Our response to any play is grounded in an awareness of the power and process of the actor, a sense of what he is doing and what he is. The process of acting is not to be confused with a way of pointing to figures in the world, as if to say, "Here is a Danish prince, here is a Brooklyn salesman." It is a special way of possessing these figures, and it arouses characteristic feelings and perceptions. The actor's way of coming at the objects of his imitation, his use of his own body as the immediate means of his art, creates a special response in his audience. Acting explores the world for us in a unique way, and drama is an extension, a fulfilling of that mode of exploration, a testing of its boundaries. The power of the actor has to do with the allure and difficulty of the actor's process, the inherent claim that bodily imitation makes on its audience's minds and lives.

Whom do we see when we watch a play? The actor establishes before us a particularly interesting and energetic human being, who is not simply the actor and not properly the character, but the actor-as-character, to whom we relate in a special way. Precisely how we relate to him is a subject we will be pursuing, in one form or another, throughout this book, but at this stage a few preliminary indications may help. This extraordinary personage, the actor-as-character, will be more interesting than people usually are in ordinary life; but he will be different from them in other ways too. He will *command* our interest more; he will be more definitely projected. He will be more intimately in touch with us than most "real" people and yet more removed, safer somehow and yet more vulnerable, more *ours* in some way and yet less our responsibility, more privileged than most, yet at our pleasure, more attractive and more equivocal, more liberated and more constrained. All told, if the actor is competent, there is bound to be something unusual and riveting about the actor-as-character, whatever the role may be. There will be a compelling strangeness about him, the presence, I would suggest, of that strange energy I referred to earlier, the energy which is other-than-mimetic. In the rest of this chapter, I shall be trying to describe more fully what this strangeness is like and where it comes from, as well as some of the ways it makes itself felt in the roles, actions, and effects of drama.

* * *

Since it will be useful to have a name for the energy which defines the actor's art, I shall refer to it as "terrific" energy, bearing in mind that word's root suggestion of the awesome and fearful, of manifestations both exciting and terrible. The term is appropriate for a number of reasons. First, the quality of being that an actor manifests in performance is by everyday standards not only unusual, but would in fact be quite disturbing, perhaps even frightening, if encountered outside the theater. Next, the power he exerts over our attention has something aversive or dangerous as well as attractive about it. Finally, there are important connections between the experience of acting (both ours and the actor's) and our more general experience of fear, apprehension, or terror.

The terrific aspect of acting cannot finally be separated from the mimetic. It is the natural result of the kind of mimesis the actor performs. Here let me very briefly gather together some of the reasons for the fear or strangeness or *terribilità* which enters into the actor's power over the audience. Many of the points I shall touch on will claim our attention at greater length later, but at this moment I want simply to indicate the range and

significance of the feelings that flow into the "terrificness" of acting.

1. A crucial point in the psychology of imitation is that
we are drawn to imitate objects toward whom intensely
ambivalent emotions obtain. In their extensive survey of
children's games, Iona and Peter Opie note that the most
popular *acting* games center on frightening figures and
events. Throughout history, outbreaks of mass hysteria
have typically been accompanied by mass impersonation
—as in the case of maenadism or possession by the devil.
The shaman—that tribal healer and mage whose professional activities are always histrionic—impersonates the
spirits who hold power of life and death over his tribe; he
acts out his own dangerous encounters with them,
playing all the parts. Impersonation of the dead—with the
explicit aim of appeasing what is acknowledged to be the
dead's intense hostility toward the living—is common to
most primitive cultures. Indeed it is so ubiquitous and
elaborately rendered into ceremony and scenario that it
would be reasonable to suppose it provides an actual
source for much of the drama we know.

2. If imitation is itself psychologically related to fear,
there has also been something approaching fear or awe in
society's feeling toward actors. Certainly there is a history of apprehension and condemnation. The actor has
always been considered suspect and fascinating, his
theater a place of dangerous freedom, a breeding spot for
vice, plague, and subversion, if only because of the actor's
power to assemble an audience. More than that, the
actor's art has always seemed a kind of provocation.
Simply by his willingness to take on a gait, voice, and
costume that are not "his own," the actor has appeared to
pose a threat to the order of things, a challenge to the
decent limits of being. There is something inherently
profligate in his enterprise. And this opinion has not been

confined to the order-loving authorities and the gossip-loving masses. To philosophers and moralists from Plato on, the actor has seemed guilty of what one critic has very aptly called "ontological subversiveness." A man is supposed to have only *one* being; what kind of creature can shift identities at will?

3. Beyond this, there is a kind of uncanniness about acting, akin to the uncanniness of the mask—a mingling of the animate and the inanimate, a projection of human energy beyond normal bounds, as in mediumship or ventriloquism. While on stage, the actor enjoys a kind of omnipotence, a privilege and protection not unlike that accorded sacred beings—whatever he is doing, whatever crimes he may appear to commit, he is not to be interfered with. Yet at the same time he seems abnormally exposed, abnormally dependent upon us. And if primitive drama can usually be interpreted as the impersonation of spirits, especially spirits of the dead, there is likewise always something ghostly or haunting about an actor. Part of his strangeness corresponds exactly to the kind Freud describes in his essay on the uncanny—it arouses a fearful sense that aggressions we ordinarily suppress are walking in the world.

4. How do you imitate an actor? By what crude familiar signs can his quality be made known? Mark Twain's Duke of Bilgewater goes to work this way:

> *He told us to give attention. Then he strikes a most noble attitude, with one leg shoved forwards, and his arms stretched away up, and his head tilted back, looking up at the sky; and then he begins to rip and rave and grit his teeth; and after that, all through his speech he howled, and spread around, and swelled up his chest, and just knocked the spots out of any acting ever I see before.*

This is a parody of nineteenth-century acting at its grandiloquent extreme, but we need not be historical scholars to recognize the portrait. It is a caricature not only of one style but of acting in general. The unspecified but intense "possession," the strained body, the frantic movements crudely and ludicrously reflect a defining element: an aggressive and haunting energy passing through the performer, changing his personality, and being transmitted to his audience. The bad actor of course has to signal what the good actor simply can make us feel, but the caricature acknowledges the psychic strangeness, the departure from ordinary life, that acting, however naturalistic or subdued, always suggests. From the histrionic attitudes preserved in Greek vase painting to the traditional gestures of the Noh, from the "teapot stance" of the eighteenth century to the Actors' Studio crouch, some outward expression of that strangeness has always appeared. Our parodies of acting point to our awareness of the terrific energy present in performance. A well-known portrait of Garrick shows him as Hamlet, stepping back in fright from his father's apparition, in an attitude Bilgewater might have envied. The moment the artist has chosen, one of Garrick's most celebrated effects, is archetypally "dramatic," a full flowering of the strangeness of acting. Garrick, in this scene, is letting loose the kind of power we always expect an actor to be capable of, however subtly or obliquely he may exercise it—and Garrick was famous for his refinement. The great actor has always been able to convince us he has seen a ghost, and in so doing to frighten us as if he were one himself. Indeed, ghosts and drama are intimately related, as we shall see later.

* * *

The power of the actor may well remind us of his primitive prototypes. He retains something of the strangeness and freedom of a man painted in blood and dressed in animal skins, howling at the moon, a shaman healing his tribe by allowing himself to be torn apart and reassembled by the spirits who possess his body, the leader of the maenad rout who is at once a sacrifice and a god. Whatever primitive images he may suggest, the energy he projects by being other-than-himself is fundamental to the nature of his art. He is a figure of fear or awe, and of extraordinary delight, by virtue of his skills, whose power is felt throughout the audience—and must be felt if we are to respond well to his acting, whatever the "accuracy" of his "portrayal" may be. He is beyond us because he is disguised; he both is and is not himself. The actor's body is possessed by something other, that is at once the particular object of his mimesis and a vaguer, more numinous source. I would say that it corresponds to otherness itself in its threatening aspect, all that generality of terror man has tried, apparently from his earliest days, to enact so as to control.

* * *

I am not suggesting of course that there is something scary about every actor in every play. I do insist that all the qualities of dramatic performance draw upon a transformation, a handling of fearful materials, and that a residual uncanniness contributes to the impression every actor makes, even if this is felt as charm, strength, authority, humor, arrestingness, or what we usually mean by "skill"—and the skill may be that of the Actors' Studio or the Berliner Ensemble. Whatever his stylization, whatever his distance from the part, the actor passes into a mode of being that draws strength from a confrontation with the fearful, from the assumption of qualities that cut against the "natural."

Suppose I see a man coming toward me down the beach and I quickly begin to imitate him. Is there any fear in this? Say I am not frightened by him, at least in any conscious sense—and let us not assume any unconscious fear either. Sheer ebullience, interest in him or in imitation, would seem to be the spring. But even in this pure example, what I am doing not only implies but creates a powerfully ambivalent relation. I am incorporating something other, reacting to the existence of someone else by becoming him. It is a combination of submission and control, a reaction to his otherness and his impingement upon me. It is kin to voodoo and Arctic hysteria. And whatever its cause, it cannot be said to *look* entirely friendly. My being, through the changes my body is assuming, is moving away from this man and toward him, away from and in extension of myself. Physically, I am becoming more like him, less like myself; but by doing so I am hiding myself from him. I am calling attention to both of us and to our relation, yet I am blocking the channels through which normal human relations flow. If he were to notice what I am doing, he would not be delighted. Whether or not "unconscious fear" is active in my example, certainly response as if to threat is. The point, then, is not that all imitation is a manifestation of fright, but that imitation is deeply related to the roots of fear, that it is a way of handling what we think of as fear's sources, those spirits, aggressions, ghosts, others—call them by what metaphysical name we will—that haunt our world from infancy.

* * *

The community's treatment of actors has alternated between veneration, as in Greece and Japan, and persecution, as in Elizabethan England and China; more important, it has usually contained elements of both. Actors in historical times tend to be treated as the spirits of the dead or sacrificial victims are treated by primitive cultures. The community focuses on them, makes them a cynosure, enjoys seeing them dressed up in their proper costumes at the proper times. But always the attraction springs from and exists in tension with an implied hostility. Expulsion or destruction hovers about them. A hint of shame and relish lies in the audience's solicitude. They are elevated above the community by the role they take on, but their elevation exposes them; they serve at their audience's pleasure. The roles playwrights devise for actors in the theater are like those we devise for them in the juicier gossip columns and those our ancestors devised in ritual and sacrifice—they engage a double impulse of attraction and repulsion. We come together to adore their fearful energies, to be infected by their risks and recklessness, to enjoy what happens to them. And the actors feel the same double impulse toward us, which in turn becomes part of what we feel as we watch them mastering their audience. Our reaction to them heightens the double impulse, drives it toward a point of tension. We are at once the risk the actors run and the immense body of pleasure they control, a wave of threat and promise constantly beating against their performance, bringing it to life.

The double impulse that acting arouses is central to all drama. It is present even in the elementary form of impersonation found in maenadism—the ecstatic dancing, common to so many cultures, that forms the basis for the worship of Dionysus. Dionysus is the proper god of the theater—not because drama derives from the worship of Dionysus (modern scholarship has shown this to be a highly questionable proposition), but because to worship Dionysus is to begin to act. Like the shaman in his trance, the Dionysiac celebrant in his ecstasy is a prototype of the actor. His transport carries him into impersonation. He abandons his own personality and adopts another, expressing this by radical changes in dress, carriage, expression, and behavior. He acts the god and acts his followers and enemies; eventually he is likely to act the god's story—of mutilation and resurrection, persecution and triumph; always he acts the threat to the individual that Dionysus represents and the promise he extends.

Dionysus may be described as everything mysterious in the outside world that threatens to overwhelm the individual and every impulse in the individual that longs to be free of the limits the world imposes—"the principle of animal life," as one scholar puts it, *"Tauros* and *Taurophagos,* the hunted and the hunter—the unrestrained potency which man envies in the beasts and seeks to assimilate." The Dionysiac celebrant is at once both hunter and animal, acting out impulses that are both exalting and terrifying. The exhilaration of this worship is double; it is to taste the madness of acting and the madness of theatergoing at once. The celebrants form an ecstatic, dancing group, at once performers and audience, sealed off and yet satisfyingly beheld in their rapture, a kind of theater commune. They are dangerously centripetal in their effect on outsiders, drawing them in—as Euripides' Pentheus discovers—with the desire both to behold and to perform.

The figures of Dionysus and his great enemy, Pentheus, easily emerge from the pre-dramatic revel of the maenads because they are already implicit, as hunter and victim, in what the maenads express. Pentheus tries to hunt Dionysus down, but he is lured into the celebration against his will. Dionysus manifests his power by destroying him. And Euripides again has a telling point to make about the nature of drama when he makes his Pentheus and Dionysus much more alike than they imagine themselves to be. Each is arrogant, tyrannical, and self-indulgent. Pentheus is fascinated by the mysteries of Dionysus, though he ruthlessly attempts to stamp them out. Dionysus, for all his flowing locks and languid appearance, is equally ruthless in punishing his enemies. If Dionysus is the eventual easy victor (in Euripides, he is a little outside the action as compared to Pentheus and the Theban maenads), we nevertheless do see him imprisoned and manhandled; and we do remember that, earlier in his career, he has been torn to pieces (by older gods) and reassembled, as Pentheus finally is. The roles of Pentheus and Dionysus require—as does every major dramatic part—that the actor embody the double impulse of the revel: the ecstasy of power over others and the ecstasy of self-surrender.

Not only is this double impulse present in any major dramatic role (and to some extent in any role), its presence always shapes the audience's expectations. The actor-as-character is a godlike figure who in some sense defies the gods, becomes vulnerable to them. But if, because of his power and daring, he is always in some way attractive to us, it is also true that we always come to the theater to see him destroyed. This applies as much to Jack Worthing as to Oedipus. For if we see in the hero of *The Importance of Being Earnest* a dandy of breathtaking insouciance and triviality, a monstrous infant with the *mana* of a perfect gentleman, who eats muffins with a perfection of self-indulgence that our body responds to by imitating at the first available opportunity (watch us at intermission with an orange drink in our hand) and if, still, this figure is caught up in a plot that brings pressures of embarrassment and awkwardness to bear exactly at his points of dandiacal recklessness and strength, if his efforts to be Ernest in town and Jack in the country grow so complicated that they finally threaten to make him look quite silly—if we watch him being out-insouzianced and out-self-indulged, even at a climactic point out-muffined—we feel a superb justness and wholeness in the dramatic design that allows for all this. But it is a justness and wholeness that proceeds from the terrificness, the essential liberation and exposure, of acting itself. Worthing's delightful insouciance demands that the farce attack him. Our expectations, and our satisfactions when they are fulfilled, spring from the double impulse aroused by acting.

* * *

There is always a chorus. There is always a play-within-the-play. Eric Bentley has observed that Pirandello regularly reproduces the situation of a Sicilian village—"a center of suffering and a periphery of busybodies"; and John Holloway has noticed that at some point in every Shakespearean tragedy the hero encounters a crowd that both respects and threatens him; and in his *Orestes* Euripides slyly gives the solicitous chorus of Argive women some attributes of the persecuting Furies—but the overriding fact is that a dramatic hero is always surrounded by a social group, actual or implied, who press upon him with extraordinary attention, extraordinary threat, just as the audience in the theater does. Even in one-character plays—*On the Harmfulness of Tobacco*, *Before Breakfast*, *The Human Voice*, *Hello Out There*, *Krapp's Last Tape*—the character must direct his remarks to a real or imagined audience whom he makes take on a choral role.

In a way, the on-stage audience is not only a surrogate for the off; it seems almost to free us from any emotion toward the actor that might seriously disrupt the performance, from the violence we would ordinarily expect to feel if we were a potential mob confronted by a provocative stranger. In the theater the potential violence of the audience, the destructive focus natural to any group, is both aroused and appeased, but the play itself works to indulge it. We are not violent toward the actor (at least while his acting pleases). But *it* is violent; somewhere in every play something threatens to tear the principal character apart.

∗　∗　∗

Chorus and main actor manage in any play to re-enact the defining peculiarities of the actor's art. Dramatic character always recapitulates and rides on, draws energy from, the essential strangeness and fascination of an actor for those who gather to watch him perform. In any good play, the principal characters go beyond ordinary bounds in ways that remind us of acting. They are capable of some kind of seductive, hypnotic, or commanding expression, mixing aggression and exposure in a way for which the community presented in the play can scourge them. This is not only true of Tamburlaine and Blanche Dubois and Dionysus; even the thoroughly nice Rosalind of *As You Like It* is such a figure, with her boy's clothes and attacking wit, her power over those around her, her exposed position in the court, her unprotected flight to the forest, her danger and her energy and daring. In comedy, of course, the scourge is either avoided or diverted, the sense of extremism disguised (some techniques will be considered in the next chapter), but the exposure and aggression, the seduction and attack, the ontological subversiveness remain. The characters of drama are actors.

∗　∗　∗

The theory and criticism of the drama have been marked by a recurrence of what might be called polar formulas, that is, formulas which use systems of paired opposites to describe features of plot and character present in important works and genres. One thinks of Aristotle's pity and terror, the pathos/theophany of the Cambridge School, or the "complementarity" principle recently put forward by Norman Rabkin. These differ from the "ambiguities" of literature in that they do not describe multiplicity of reference or of levels of meaning—though these of course may also be present in drama—but doubleness of response. I would suggest they all derive from the response inherent in the actor-audience encounter. Furthermore role, plot, action, all the major elements of dramatic design, may best be understood as ways of sustaining and extending the actor's contact with his audience, of intensifying and enriching it, especially of associating it in our minds with various strands of our experience outside the theater—of letting an actor be what we want him, perhaps need him to be.

∗　∗　∗

Aristotle's *Poetics* is, intermittently, a profound contribution to the psychology of art, and it finds its own way to the central importance of the relation between audience and actor. The famous discussion of the tragic hero's character is not an attempt to establish limits according to a moral prescription—to say only these attributes should be admitted because others are bad for the soul—but to grasp the role of moral attitudes in the dynamics of audience response. Aristotle's psychology may be too rational, and his moral reading of the world may limit his awareness of possible responses. He does not acknowledge, for example, the extent to which "bad" characters and "evil" acts arouse "tragic" emotions. But he is crucially aware that we have to be both attracted and repelled—the more so the better—or some vital element in our interest will go slack. Who is the ideal hero he describes, the good but not perfect man, compromised by the elusive *hamartia* ("It is not through wickedness and vice that he falls into misfortune, but through some *hamartia*")? He is simply the kind of person to whom we can remain exaltingly drawn while discovering fearful things about him. Attempts to explicate this passage—

which has always proved something of a mystery to scholars—have hinged on elaborate definitions of *hamartia*. But these, by misunderstanding the psychological orientation of Aristotle's analysis, have missed the linguistic role *hamartia* plays in his formula. No satisfyingly explicit definition of *hamartia* will ever be found, because the impulse behind the search for such a definition is to find a fact about the word which will explain the other terms in the tragic formula; while Aristotle seems to have chosen *hamartia* (which in other contexts has such plain but noncommittal meanings as "wide of the mark") as the best name for exactly that quality which would allow the rest of the formula to operate. *Hamartia* is thus simply the whatever-it-is, the askewness of character, that allows us to feel the hero is, by nature, in some way significantly related to his fate, without our ceasing to be significantly attached to him.

Because this felt askewness invites a variety of conflicting interpretations when it occurs (it may be taken as a moral deficiency, a flaw in the universe, a piece of rotten luck, part of a divine plan, or whatever), moral puzzles have tended to spring up around the heads of great dramatic heroes, particularly in tragedy. As such, they have often roused interminable—because unresolvable—critical debates as to the culpability of characters like Agamemnon, Hippolytus, Hamlet, Othello, Alceste in *The Misanthrope*, and Master Builder Solness. It should always be borne in mind that such debates are far more likely to be signs of the power of the plays concerned than descriptions of their meaning. The character of any great dramatic hero, analyzed carefully enough, is likely to prove a moral puzzle, because it has been designed to promote and exploit conflicting responses.

Aristotle may well have been convinced that the hero could not exceed certain limits of guilt and innocence at either end of a restricted spectrum. Certainly he does not appear to consider what might be called reverse *hamartia*, that twist of character that makes a clearly evil figure commanding or in some way sympathetic—Clytemnestra's grim patience or Macbeth's moral imagination. Nevertheless, he manages to seize on the phenomenon that our relation with a dramatic hero thrives on opposed responses. *Hamartia* is an especially useful word because it shades off so easily into condemnation or exculpation (we translate its appearance in the Greek of the New Testament as "sin"; Aristotle himself uses it in the *Ethics* to characterize mere "errors," committed through ignorance or inadvertence); thus, it brings together in a single moral term the polarities of feeling the actor-as-hero arouses.

* * *

The playwright will try to find the actor roles in which hunter and victim are one, in which pity and terror, or allure and repulsion, or appeal and attack are mingled. His aim is to turn the actor loose, to let him make the liveliest connection possible with his audience's fears and desires. That is, he will try to discover what, in the audience's own life, this doubleness of response, this feeling of actorly strangeness, can be strikingly connected to. Even in a culture without playwrights or formal drama, there will be a pressure toward inventing public performances that associate the appetite for acting with the deep fears and desires of the community. This may help explain how "ritual forms" are related to dramatic experience. We are clearly indebted to the great Cambridge anthropologists for the discovery of remarkable parallels between sophisticated drama and the rituals by which primitive societies mark the triumph of the new year over the old. These have had a profound influence on our way of thinking about literature and drama. But the influence has tended to be misleading in its suggestion that the ritual pattern is in some sense a cause, formal or historical, of the dramatic design. There is certainly no hard evidence for this. Indeed, it would seem more reasonable to trace both ritual and drama to a common source—to a desire or need to elaborate the experience of bodily mimesis, the experience of someone changing his personality before an audience; the desire to make use of this experience, to enjoy the social group's highly charged relation with the performer, and to make that relation and that excitement stand for as much as possible in the group's experience of life, especially as a way of dealing with fear. Sacrificial or seasonal ritual reflects and draws on the doubleness and power of the actor-audience relation—out of which relation the ritual may be presumed to grow, just as drama does. The theory of ritual origins derives drama from human sacrifice or fertility ritual. The hero, we are told, descends from the sacred victim, the action from the combat between winter and spring. However, both the sacrificial victim and the tragic hero may be seen as versions of the actor-as-character. They both perform for an audience, put aside their own personalities, dress up; they identify with something powerful and take on its power by impersonation; at the same time they become victims of the very power they enact. They are venerated and torn apart because they impersonate something invulnerable, something beyond themselves. Until the moment of sacrifice, the victim, like the actor-as-character, is phenomenologically immortal, immune from interference while he plays his part. The "ritual outlines" of drama, then, are not evidence of priority, but marks of common ancestry—one might speak with equal accuracy of the "dramatic outlines" of ritual. If the career of the year-king and the outcry of those who surround him parallel the action and emotions of tragedy, it is not because one derives from the other, but because both are elaborations of the fear and attraction on which acting builds. The actor, like the ritual victim, is always a candidate for being torn apart (*sparagmos*); the plots of comedy and tragedy agree in this. Drama and *sparagmos* are not historically but psychologically related. Climactic discovery, lament and exaltation are the issue of the tragic pattern not because they are ritual fossils, deriving from the recognition and theophany that attend a divine hero's mutilation and resurrection, but because they are natural to the tragic pattern. The actor-as-character thrusts forward his fascinating, other-than-human identity against the destructive pressures of the plot, which are designed to help him do so, and when he dies, we know that he will be resurrected because he is an actor. Indeed, he will mime repeated dyings and risings in his bow, that gesture of submission which is also a thrust toward the audience. Like the related tradition of applauding the audience, the bow symbolizes that combination of aggression and reception we find everywhere in the actor-audience exchange.

* * *

Any playwright, actor, or director knows that aggression is an essential ingredient of drama. But not perhaps for the reasons familiarly proposed. I doubt whether it can be established that "conflict" is in some way essentially dramatic. I think, rather, the importance of aggression has more to do with the aggression the actor himself must use to assume his role and to maintain contact with his audience. The effort to set actors loose, to harness and encourage their terrific energies, requires a play of aggression that must be felt in every turn of dialogue, in every corner of the play.

Aggression as a psychological concept and action as a dramatic one are both notoriously difficult to define, but, strikingly enough, the two considered together help to clarify each other. Whatever action may be, everyone will agree that it is locally felt in the line-to-line presence of a psychic thrust, an impulse within the actor pushing out against the other actors and circumstances on stage, and that the interplay of thrusts, the push and pull between actors, is what makes dialogue playable. If we think of aggression simply as this thrust, a psychic and physical energy working outward from somewhere inside the individual, looking for materials on which to make an impression, looking also for other life that will make its own life known, we can see how aggression, complexly projected but intimately and immediately received by the audience, is the stuff of drama. At least three kinds will be simultaneously present in the theater, and each will have its effect on what we feel as the "action" of the play. Most recognizable, though not necessarily most important, is the aggressive flow direct from actor to audience—the thrust outward to make connection in performance, to create and control a response. It is itself a response to the terrible challenge the audience presents, the devouring expectation or crushing indifference the actor senses *out there*. More central is the aggression involved in taking on a role, the effort with which the materials of one's own psyche and of one's own body must be rearranged to take on and in some way project a character—that is, to thrust this other presence into the already aggressive flow of performance. Finally there is aggression within the action of the play itself—and this, though generally recognized, is often misunderstood. The aggression of the plot is not the result of some dramatic law requiring struggle, debate, event, emphasis—all of which can be quite undramatic. It springs from the other aggressions—the aggressions of impersonation and performance. The plot must offer the actor's aggressive energy (and the related aggressive energy of the audience) ample and interesting scope. The effort of the actor to act and the pleasures that acting generates are perceived as part of the action of the play, which forms their field.

* * *

Later in this book we shall consider some of the ways in which dramatic action grows out of the processes of performance. Here, however, I want only to call attention to a rudimentary example of the connection between the aggressions of acting and the action of drama. The text I wish to discuss is not, dramatically speaking, very remarkable, and the effect in question is almost microscopic; but for just these reasons it has a special interest. It nicely marks the transition from a ceremony that is not drama to one that is; and the most striking difference between the two ceremonies is the addition of an odd, apparently gratuitous charge of aggression.

The earliest certain record we have of dramatic production in medieval Europe is contained in the *Regularis Concordia* of Ethelwold, Bishop of Winchester, in the tenth century. It is a brief and extremely simple dramatization of the Gospel scene in which the three Marys meet the Angel at the sepulchre and learn that Christ has risen. The immediate source of the dialogue is in dispute, but it is clearly associated with the Masses and related ceremonies of the Roman church at Easter time, and derives ultimately from Matthew 28:1–8 and Mark 16:2–7. The drama is usually called *Quem Quaeritis*, after its opening words. The Catholic Mass, of course, is a symbolic ritual whose participants, appropriately costumed, refer in their actions to a familiar narrative and sacred allegory. All this is in a sense "dramatic," but only in a sense—and one which can actually be quite misleading. For though the Mass has scenes and characters, spectacle and performance, recognitions and peripeties, it is not, properly speaking, histrionic. The officiant may symbolize an eternal prototype; he may make the sacred figure or event present to the congregation; he may stand for Christ, who may even—to use doctrinal language—be "really present" during the ceremony; but he does not enact what he represents. The priest is not an actor, the Mass is not a play. To confuse the two is to miss the significance of the *Quem Quaeritis*, which by the slightest of adjustments converts the ritual to drama and its officiants to actors. In the Mass, the priest represents Christ *by virtue of his office*, and not through any exercise of his individual sensibility or cunning. In the *Quem Quaeritis*, however, the participants represent the Marys and the Angel by *acting*—and Ethelwold is full of suggestions on how to give a convincing performance. It is the presence of acting that distinguishes the *Quem Quaeritis* play from the "ritual drama" of the Mass and from other ceremonial spectacles like the so-called Egyptian Coronation Play. The *Quem Quaeritis*, it is true, may not be the first instance of genuine drama in the medieval church. There is some evidence that a histrionic element was already creeping into the ceremonial during the ninth century—though it is impossible to tell how sustained or even how complete the enactment was. Nonetheless, Ethelwold's description is the earliest we have, and it does allow us to see a passage which is clearly ceremonial in origin transformed into something which is definitely histrionic. To me, the most significant thing about Ethelwold's account is that it introduces a little movement of aggression quite foreign to the undramatized version of the text, and equally foreign to the Gospel account on which the dialogue is based. I think it is a natural outgrowth of the energy of impersonation, and certainly represents a natural impulse to "dramatize" the scene. Into a text that, in the Gospel account or the sung tropes of the medieval

Mass, is simply a celebration, Ethelwold (or his unknown source) inserts a push and pull, a clash of directions. The Angel tells the women to announce that Christ has risen; then, having set the Marys moving away in praise, he calls them back for further revelations:

> At the word of his bidding let those three [the Marys] turn to the choir and say, Alleluia! resurrexit Dominus! [Alleluia! The Lord has risen!] This said, let the one still sitting there and as if recalling them, say the anthem Venite et videte locum [Come and see the place].

In the Gospels, the Angel calls on the women to inspect the tomb *before* commanding them to say that Christ has risen. The shift in sequence and the "as if recalling them" create an important change. The Angel sets them off in one direction, then reaches out and gives them an opposing command, which pulls them back. This push and pull is an elementary requirement of dramatic dialogue, and involves the actor-as-Angel in a type of attack the celebrant of the Mass never needs or makes. It springs, I would suggest, from the strangeness of acting, from the natural aggression of histrionic performance itself.

* * *

The question of aggression in drama leads us back to the subject of ghosts. First some preliminary observations.

Primitive thought regularly associates the following ideas: aggression; otherness; spirits (including ghosts and other spirits of the dead); sacred beings; and impersonation.

The Kaingang of Brazil have the same word for:

differences of any kind;
men from rival groups;
Brazilians, who are their enemy;
the dead and all mythical, demonic, or divine beings.

Primitive man pictures himself surrounded by a malevolent chaotic externality. The outside world, everything beyond the consecrated precincts inhabited by the tribe, is understood to be peopled with aggressive ghosts. The ghost gives this externality a shape something like man's own, which far from domesticating the threat, serves merely to evoke its menace. Primitive religion, like modern psychology, recognizes that the threatening otherness we sense beyond our limits corresponds to something at work inside us.

* * *

Drama probably began with ghosts, with prehistoric impersonations intended to transfigure the malice of spirits—to indulge, placate, or wrestle with the dead, to turn Furies into Eumenides. "Nothing is more dramatic than a ghost," says T. S. Eliot in an early essay. He then drops the subject; but the relation we have been pursuing between dramatic action, aggression, and the peculiar psychic energy of the actor's art will be illuminated if we stop to ask why. Ghosts are dramatic because they make for action. By their very nature they stimulate the flow of aggression on which all drama depends. Ghosts haunt us; that is, they bring aggression to bear on us in an especially volatile way—a way that penetrates with particular intensity to our psyche and encourages imitation, encourages us to haunt as we are haunted. They are hard to defend against; they cannot easily be subdued or ignored. They create an unstable situation in the external world because their victims must transfer their aggressions to new objects. When a real person hits us we can either hit him back or refuse to. Either reaction may make for drama, but the exchange can easily be enclosed, a balance quickly restored. We can't hit back at a ghost, however, any more than we can ignore him. The haunting transmits itself through us to a wider world. Thus the classical device of a ghost crying for revenge precipitates the great Elizabethan discoveries as to plot and action— perhaps the greatest discovery being that the ghost could be internalized in the figure of the revenger, who could then be fully human—and a starring part—while retaining a ghost's peculiar interest and privileges. The ghost makes easy and intense a kind of psychic thrust and counterthrust that connects inner states of feeling—desire, fear, hatred—with movement and change in the external world, the transformation, essential to drama, of activity into action.

Our relation to a ghost—or the relation of the characters on stage to a ghost—recapitulates much of the essential relation between audience and actor, especially the fusion, so noticeable in that relation, of impressive distance with impressive intimacy. Like the actor-as-character on his stage, the ghost is a kind of sacred being (privileged, invulnerable, held in awe, free of ordinary limits) manipulating our responses. He is like us, but changed. He has the power to move us deeply, but we cannot make direct contact with him, because he inhabits another world. He is so untouchable he seems to be inside us.

A theory of ghosts might in itself make a good theory of drama, and the historical version of this theory might note that at about the time when audiences cease to believe in ghosts they begin to be haunted by memories. People have always had memories, of course, but I would suggest that they are not *haunted* by memories much before Rousseau. In any historical period, drama must find its proper ghosts, sources for haunting that an audience can accept as both meaningful and mysterious. These need not be anthropomorphic—it is necessary only that we believe in them. Today, for example, we are haunted by unconscious memories as well as conscious ones; by our childhoods, our bodies, our institutions; by money and class; by race and sexuality; by a century of doubts as to the limits of human freedom. These are the ghosts that walk the modern stage, a surprising number of them first set walking there by Ibsen.

* * *

Writers on the theater frequently speak of events or characters in a play as if they were fictions in the novelistic sense, things *represented* by actors as imagined events may be represented by words or pictures. This is an especially pernicious instance of the literary-mimetic heritage, deriving ultimately from Aristotle's casual bracketing of theatrical mimesis with other kinds; but it seems to be committed as much by avant-garde critics, whose avowed concerns are anti-literary, as by more conservative ones. Indeed, this circumstance suggests how powerful and insufficiently examined the literary-mimetic tradition is. Here is Richard Schechner, for example, surely one of the best-informed and most interesting observers we have of experimental performance and performance theory, trying to describe what he sees as a new immediacy in contemporary theater practice:

> We conventionally think of "process" as the sequence of events in the script. . . . Thus the "death" of Hamlet or the "blinding" of Oedipus. When I think of process, I think of something that occurs in fact here and now: the melting of the ice-liths in Fluids, the dodging and ultimate taking of spears in the Tiwi Trial, the dancing of the hevehe.

He contrasts the immediacy, the here-and-now quality of a contemporary happening (which he links to examples of primitive ritual and drama) with what he considers the story-telling of *Hamlet* or *Oedipus Rex*. Now, there are differences between a Kaprow happening and a play by

Shakespeare or Sophocles (though the Orokolo hevehe ritual he refers to is different from both), but they do not have to do with immediacy. The remoteness Schechner finds in conventional drama exists only in conventional, i.e. literary, thought about drama—not in the plays themselves. For me, Hamlet never refers to Elsinore or to a certain character whom I discover through the medium, as I discover a character in a novel through words. There are, to be sure, "events" in the script, and it is a useful task to distinguish them from the events in *Fluids* or the Tiwi trial by combat; but when the play is performed the events are not in the past, not "elsewhere," any more than Hamlet himself is. They are here and now on stage.

When Clifton Davis steps out from behind his desk to sing "Love's Revenge" in *Two Gentlemen of Verona* at the St. James, we don't look through his song to an event in the script or to Shakespeare's London. (By the time this appears the show will no longer be running, but the present tense is important.) We look at the actor, we respond to his voice and body and words. We do not use his gesture and language to imagine "Valentine in Milan" as we would do if these were the symbols in a book. We respond to the beat and the drive of his being—to what they make happen around him on the stage—and to the waves of his bodily presence as they beat against us and rebound to him. This is as here-and-now as any block of ice melting.

I've chosen an electric moment in a recent musical comedy to emphasize my point; but the point itself is that what we respond to in Anthony Quayle's Tamburlaine or whoever's Hamlet is located as much in the here-and-now as Clifton Davis's number in *Two Gentlemen*. And when we read a script what we do, or at least what we should do if we have any familiarity with the theater, is construct in our minds not a scene in old Verona or Elsinore or

Thebes but a scene on a stage before an audience here and now.

There is another reason why I've chosen this "popular" example. The situation of musical comedy with its strong and simple beats of bodily vigor, the clear arousal of the audience, the uniqueness of the life we experience sealing us in a particular present, a particular space—these are easier to hang on to in memory than recollections of famous plays we have often read and read about. This is not primarily because the dramatic situation is simpler, and certainly not because it is different, but because we are likely to remember this kind of theatrical occasion more accurately. It will hold out better against the abstract tide of aesthetic theory based on literature, which washes us away from our true memories of theatrical experience whenever we try to think about classics that are so often the subjects of theory, like our well-thumbed *Hamlet*. But the experience is in essence the same. It is experience of performance, of the actor's mimesis, of a man going beyond himself, taking on a new personality and wrapping us in the power of that transformation as it occurs.

In the article I've quoted from, Schechner attempts to distinguish between conventionally scripted drama and a class of performances he calls "actuals." His observations are useful, but his controlling notion of the relation of text to performance is suffused with exactly those literary ideas of mimesis his feeling for the theater rebels against:

> The goal of conventional acting and the basis of Stanislavsky's great work is to enable the actor to "really live" his character. Nature ought to be so skillfully imitated that it seems to be re-presented on the stage. The tendency of an actual is the opposite. Instead of the smooth "professionalism" of the "good actor," there are rough and unexpected turbulences,

troubled interruptions. These are not stylistic, but the genuine meeting between performer and problem.
  Two processes unfold simultaneously. The first is the one shaped by author and director, the "play" and the "mise en scène." But just as important is the more evanescent process of the performer.

Now, Schechner is making a genuine stylistic distinction between actuals and other dramatic events (though I think he exaggerates and romanticizes the intensity and interest of the turbulences available to the unscripted performer—and misses the fact that ritual sequences like the hevehe cycle are usually "scripted" to a staggering degree). But he goes astray in the kind of separation he insists on—here and elsewhere—between what the performer shows us and what the "play" shows us. Any dramatic text finds its proper life through performance. It exists in order to be performed, in order to become fully available to, fully expressed by "the more evanescent process of the performer." The process of the performer is implicit in the great texts, and it is part of their meaning. When we read *Hamlet* it is to discover—to approximate in our imaginations—what under ideal conditions that evanescent process might be like.

Ironically enough, Schechner's distinction between the immediacy of the performer and that of the play, though "anti-literary" in bias, actually has its roots in a distinctly literary view of drama. A clue to this may be found in the passage quoted above, where he describes traditional acting as "re-presentation"—that is, a reconstitution before our eyes of a Nature whose original is conceived to be outside the theater. This is nothing but the standard literary notion of acting again—here is the way old Hamlet of Elsinore walked and talked. Given the ease with which he slips into this literary way of thinking about acting, it is no wonder that Schechner should treat the actor's text as "re-presentational," and believe that the "events" in the script are less here-and-now than the actor's performance. One can scarcely blame Schechner for being influenced by a commonplace of dramatic theory that is at least as old as Aristotle. But we should note that it is just this inadequate, literature-derived critical tradition that has encouraged Schechner, like Artaud before him, to think of all scripted drama as literary. I am afraid that much contemporary production and criticism, particularly of Shakespeare and other classics, is an attempt to "rescue" plays from a deadening literariness which often can be located squarely in the minds of the rescuers themselves.

I am not out to poke fun at serious attempts in the confused field of the poetics of drama. If it is confused, it is because the evanescent process of performance is immensely elusive and our means for talking about it are derived from centuries of discussion based almost exclusively on literature. Every passionate effort to describe the phenomenology of drama helps us at this stage of our knowledge—even in the confusions it stumbles upon. For instance, I think Schechner is quite right to note two processes working together in scripted drama, and there is a kind of rough justice in associating one with the play and one with the performer. That is, we're aware of things in the play pushing at or going on around or outside the performer—plot, for instance, the presence of conventions or prior exposition, the pressure of our manipulated expectations. These may play against what the performer does and what we feel about him, creating effects of strong and subtle opposition. While Hamlet deliberates whether to kill the King at prayer, Shakespeare's play, by the tensions of expectation it has set up, is pushing us in two directions at once. It pushes us to be aware that the killing of Claudius can't take place *yet*, can't happen this way (we expect it to be saved for the finale, for one thing)—but it also pushes us to *want* Claudius to be killed. And while we laugh at the partially improvised comedy of Falstaff in a performance of *Henry IV* we know that the political circumstances the play is laying before us must severely limit the actor's natural impulse simply to keep us laughing. But these pressures are also part of the here-and-now, the ongoing event in the theater, which constitutes the final cause of the text. They are immediate; they come to us through the performer as he performs. We take them in no differently from the way we take in the performer's posture or presence.

Schechner seems also to equate the two processes he describes with, on one hand, realism (re-presentation of nature) and something that is realism's opposite—we might call it "convention." The tension between the two is very much present in drama, and Schechner is right to call attention to it, but once again it can be understood only if we see that *both* processes are part of the unremitting immediacy of theatrical experience. All theatrical performance tends to realism, but this realism is not re-presentation of reality; it is reality itself, there before us in the theater. In a very obvious sense, what we watch in the theater is real life. Those are real people up there, who very often are doing exactly what they appear to be doing. At the same time, there is always some conventionalism. Those people are actors, and they are not doing what they appear to be doing. The actors do not behave as in real life, but their real presence inevitably lets in real action. The wall may not be real, but the door they open is a real door, the pretend victim utters a real scream and the stage kiss joins real lips and bodies. There is always an exciting tension between these literal bits of life and the make-believe.

Eliot as a young man complained of the "desert" of

literal realism into which the Elizabethan theater regrettably kept spilling its artistic vitality. His theoretical preference was for an absolute consistency of convention. This—and, I would guess, his at that point entirely literary understanding of dramatic convention and presentation—led him to suggest that *Everyman* was more perfect as a work of art than any subsequent drama. But anyone who works in the theater soon recognizes that any theatrical convention must be impure—we are always aware of the literal bits of life crowding into the picture. The more austere the convention, the further removed the play is from literal reality, the tinier the bit of real life necessary to make itself felt. Even *Everyman* is full of opportunities for the most literal and individualized rendition of fear, sorrow, entreaty, and dispute, which in performance can only intensify its allegory of the soul's confrontation with death. It is no accident that, after Eliot starts writing for the theater, we hear no more from him about the desert of realism and the importance of consistent conventions.

* * *

The art of the theater—and the nature of its appeal—cannot be separated from the mechanism of appearance and disappearance. Theater is exits and entrances. Resurrections and rehearsals, the dimming of lights, curtain calls, the curtain itself, the structure of the scene, wings, traps, the clown's head around the cardboard tree, the deus ex machina, prologues and epilogues—are all refinements and recurrences of the one pervasive motif. Wherever we have theater, we have hiding and surprise, appearance and disappearance. Among many primitive tribes, the sudden rush of the performers into the playing area and the concealment of important props and costumes are essential elements in presentation, in which the audience often actively participates:

*This stage moving is done with rather remarkable
expedition and the dancers contrive to keep the stage
furniture from the spectators' view. This attempt at
secrecy is rather noteworthy. Women spectators, for
instance, may seize their mats and rush forward to help
in concealing the stage properties as they are brought
on, already well enough concealed as they are by the
throng of stage-movers.*

Among children, games of appearance and disappearance, hiding and finding, now-you-see-it-now-you-don't are ubiquitous and powerful. And like the child's games of imitation, they spring from the experience of fear. For their purpose is twofold: to make what is lost return and to master the experience of being lost. When we are left behind—as our mothers and fathers constantly leave us—we experience not losing-someone, but being-lost. The little boy in *Beyond the Pleasure Principle* who reacts to his mother's frequent absence by developing a game in which he throws his toys under the bed is enacting losing-of-the-baby; he is mastering it, as Erik Erikson suggests. The same little boy, we recall, also played a game with his mirror, making himself appear and disappear. R. D. Laing's young daughter would make him put his hands over his eyes, then remove them and crow with delight over what she had accomplished: nothing less than her own obliteration and renewal.

Of course all works of art that unfold in time involve appearances and disappearances. Characters in a novel have their exits and entrances too. But only in the theater do actual people and objects appear, disappear, and reappear. The show goes *on*, it is repeated and rehearsed, what is lost can be brought back. Drama is full of recognitions and reconciliations, reunions and dispersals, deaths and entrances. It is not like a movie, where the product's permanence gives it an obsessive quality, as in dreams. The star dies but we can screen him indefinitely. If we need theater it's because, as we often casually say, we need "live" entertainment, and specifically because of the promise in the word "live"—it can't be dead. The immortality of the stage actor is different from that of the screen actor, who is simply preserved by a mechanical process, an indestructible illusion summoned from the past. The stage actor, while he is acting, cannot die—he must be alive. On stage, all losses can be restored.

*   *   *

Thus theater springs from the games we play with fear and loss. All art does this, but theater is closest to the root: to the shaman, the maenad, the obsessive child; to the first loomings of our parents; to ghosts and spirits; to the full physicality of the game and the apprehensions the game springs from; to the actual matter and mastery of our fears. Not that the subjects of drama are inevitably unpleasant, or that the greatest plays contain the greatest horrors. But the source of theatrical excitement lies close to our most primitive awareness of threat; the vitality of the dramatic artist springs from the inherent threatening nature of the materials he handles. Both in the process of impersonation and his relation to the audience, the actor's art never ceases to handle—with an unparalleled immediacy—the haunting volatility of a menacing world.

There is good reason why imitation of the dead, with the aim of propitiating and expelling them, is a fundamental element in so much primitive drama. Such ceremonies bring together many of drama's essentials—the impulse to act and behold acting, the mystery and appeal of exits and entrances, the dramatic excitement of ghosts, the general thrust to handle terror. And impersonating the dead has an interesting relation to aggression—a relation, we may speculate, with a significant bearing on drama. When we act out the hostile aggression of our dead toward us, we draw of course on our aggression toward them. Like the little boy in *Beyond the Pleasure Principle*, we make them go away because they have lost *us*. But by making them go away, by transforming them from malign to benevolent spirits, we also transform or banish our aggression toward them, which would otherwise remain with us undischarged. It, too, ceases to haunt us. Each year among the Tangkul of northern Burma, actors who for days have impersonated the dead, having been repeatedly feasted and heaped with gifts, are led in rich costumes and with the greatest show of respect out of their little village to a tree on the outskirts of the community—thence, it is understood, to disappear beyond the river and toward the hills, happily and forever. We may think of the *Oresteia*, which ends with a similar procession—for the Furies, before they are propitiated, feted, and renamed as the benevolent Eumenides, are themselves the threatening representatives of dead men scorned.

The transformation of ghosts, the transformation of our aggressions: In primitive mourning ritual (as in psychiatric theory) it seems impossible to separate them. Perhaps, in some useful sense, this will apply to sophisticated drama too. In the connected movements and transformations of haunting and aggression, it may be possible to discover many of the patterns and pleasures of the stage.

* * *

In thinking about aggression and action in drama, it will help not only to think about ghosts, but about figures who possess some of the attributes of ghosts, and about the way in which the power of a ghost may be passed from one character to another. I offer here one large scheme or model for this type of transaction in the hope that it may suggest other models and further applications. The literature of shamanism contains notable accounts of the reappearance, disappearance, and impersonation of the dead, accompanied by a violent struggle whose aim is to win power over the dead, or to win their power. Knud Rasmussen's description of the lifting of a storm by an Eskimo shaman is a good example, providing in clear outline a pattern that is very suggestive to the student of drama. The shaman, Horqarnaq, is possessed by a spirit:

> *At that moment there is a gurgling sound, and a helping spirit enters his body. A force has taken possession of him and he is no longer master of himself or his words. He dances, jumps, throws himself over among the clusters of the audience and cries to his dead father, who has become an evil spirit.*

Horqarnaq suddenly begins to fight with another spirit who is perhaps his father, and who seems to have entered the body of a much older colleague, Kigiuna. Horqarnaq, in a trance, also behaves like a spirit, for though he is "fighting" with spirits, he is at the same time possessed by them. He "kills" his fellow shaman three times; but then Horqarnaq himself collapses and Kigiuna in turn stands over him. The audience senses Kigiuna's new power:

> *All feel that there is a man whom death has just touched, and they involuntarily step back when, with his foot on [Horqarnaq's] chest, he turns to the audience and with astonishing eloquence announces the vision he sees.*

After a great tirade by Kigiuna, in which he describes the wind as a huge flight of naked spirits of the dead whom he promises to drive away, Horqarnaq rises and, together, hc and Kigiuna sing to the tribal gods, inducing a final vision of the spirits in full flight:

> *We saw the storm riding across the sky in the speed and thronging of naked spirits. We saw the crowd of*

*fleeing dead ones come sweeping through the billows of
the blizzard. . . .*

In the morning, they find the storm is over.

Broadly taken, the pattern illustrated in this example by
both Kigiuna and Horqarnaq—a performer wrestling
with ghosts, struggling to overcome them, perhaps being
destroyed by them, but taking on their energies in the
course of the struggle—may be felt in a vast range of
drama from the *Oresteia* to *Ghosts* to Peter Handke's
Kaspar. In partial form, it may be found in almost any
play. And in a very close parallel, the pattern recurs in a
number of Shakespearean tragedies. Shakespeare in fact
seems especially sensitive to the effect of bouts like the
one Rasmussen describes; extensive open conflicts between a ghost or some uncannily aggressive figure and a
principal character, leading to an assimilation by the hero
of some of the haunting figure's characteristics. Indeed,
the hero begins to haunt as he has been haunted.

Between Othello and Iago we have a scene that looks
like and, literally speaking, is a physical struggle, with
Othello threatening Iago and the two of them bobbing up
and down ("Do not rise yet!"). After this scene Othello
takes over Iago's interpretation of love, much of Iago's
characteristic language, and some of his hunger for
vengeance. The Fool in *King Lear* vanishes unexpectedly
in the middle of the play, but only after both his cruel
insistence on Lear's follies and his half-crazed riddling air
have been taken over by Lear himself, who earlier has
threatened the Fool with a whip and perhaps beaten him.
Apemantus haunts Timon with his misanthropy, fighting
with him till at last Timon physically drives Apemantus
away, in a scene in which he shows himself, in word and
deed, by now the more profound hater of mankind.

Above all, however, one thinks of Hamlet and his

father's ghost. Their encounter has much of the feeling, even the appearance of a struggle, with its swordplay, outbursts of savagery, the attack and retreat of Hamlet, the physical ups and downs of the Ghost. Hamlet, though finally convinced by the Ghost, seems with his sword, his agitation, his fears and his friends' fears for him, his wild and whirling words, even his mockery ("old mole") to be wrestling with an adversary—certainly the Ghost is the greatest threat of his young life. And after he has seen his father, Hamlet begins to haunt and puzzle the court of Elsinore as the Ghost has haunted and puzzled those who saw him. His actions are ambiguous, menacing yet mournful, aggressive but elusive; he calls his watchers to account. This is I, he shouts, appearing suddenly in a graveyard and using his father's title, Hamlet the Dane.

* * *

One immediate result of Hamlet's encounter with the Ghost is his antic disposition. The peculiar edge of licensed yet menacing gaiety we feel here is characteristic of a certain kind of performance style, whose scope and significance deserve more attention than they have yet received. Its methods and effects have a bearing on the whole field of comedy, and shed further light on the connection between the actor's freedom and the forms and powers of drama.

In the dramatic performances with which the Orokaiva tribesmen of Eastern New Guinea entertain themselves and their guests on important ceremonial occasions, there recurs a popular and familiar figure—the *samuna*. Grotesquely dressed, broadly clowning, aggressive and insulting, he plays a crucial role in most of the little dramas presented. Though his place in the plot and his specific role vary greatly from play to play, his manner is always the same. It is something like that of the all-licensed clown, but without any sense of relegation to a limited or subservient role. He is not only the center of the show, he is the pivot of the story. His antics are energetic, violent, often menacing, marked by wild mugging and forays into the audience.

For all its rudeness and absurdity, the part of the *samuna* carries a distinct social cachet. "I have been surprised to note," writes F. E. Williams, "that the man who takes the *samuna*'s part . . . is usually one of years, character and some importance." It has been determined that a *samuna*—the name means "the bad one"—is a spirit of the dead, what the Orokaiva call a *sovai*, or a "devil-devil." His antics and appearance clearly reflect the menace and freedom of the dead, whom Orokaiva ceremonies (of which drama is a part) seek to propitiate. What is especially interesting is the union of this menace with a comic style:

> *Altogether his aim is to make himself hideous enough for a real* binei *[another spirit], and to behave obscenely and comically enough to make his audience laugh.*

The style is specifically extravagant and aggressive— absurd, attacking, wild—just as his dress and movement are ludicrous, weird, attention-getting. This should scarcely surprise us, any more than the choice of men of standing for the role. The gaiety reflects or uses an identification—"This is the way I'd behave if I had the freedom of the dead (the way I am afraid they will behave toward me)." It is another way of escaping bodily from yourself and mastering (taking on the body of) what terrifies you.

The *samuna* is not an isolated phenomenon; he is, in varying incarnations, a familiar participant in primitive drama. We find him among the Orokolo elsewhere in New Guinea, among the Dalang of Java, and in the mummings and folk plays of Western Europe. We should in fact recognize his lineaments in that important and elusive stock-character of early English drama, the Vice—that rambunctious embodiment of impiety and malice, a seeming devil, yet one from whose trickery even the Devil himself is not exempt. Whatever the Vice's Christian significances (and though broadly clear, they are slippery) his style and the relation he sets up with the audience are clearly like the *samuna*'s. He is a grotesque, conspiratorial, hyperactive, destructive agent, blasting in among his betters, attacking us, attacking the other characters, keeping things going, making us laugh—an antic disposition taking the audience by storm.

* * *

Hamlet in the middle acts is *samuna*-like in his mixture of rudeness, disguise, disorderly appearance (down-gyved, he dresses with the characteristic menacing ludicrousness of the *sovai*), verbal and physical attack, and clownishness—all of which, as Gilbert Murray long ago pointed out, he also shares with the Orestes of legend and Euripides' play *Orestes*. Murray, of course, seized on these similarities to suggest that both roles reflect seasonal or vegetation ritual. But once again the ritual explanation would seem only to supply another parallel— and in this case at best a faint one. By focusing on the histrionic effect behind the characterization, we can become more specific about the connection between Hamlet, Orestes, the Vice, and the *samuna*—and we can do this in a way that points to the actual experience of audiences, to the distinct meaning of each role as an exploration of the world.

Most versions of the Hamlet and Orestes stories include, as Murray observes, the apparent return of the hero from the dead. The *samuna*-style seems to originate, as we have seen, in a histrionic license accorded to the dead, in the release and repugnance with which we welcome their freedom of action on the stage. Death as a subject for meditation and as a fact of life suffuses the language and plot of *Hamlet*. The prince wrestles with his ghost and puts on the antic disposition. He puts it by only after his journey to the country from whose bourn he is not supposed to return (the country of death is the audience's country, England, where the men are all as mad as he); a round trip from which he emerges in a graveyard, in yet another disposition—ready to trade jokes, yet treading carefully and patiently with two new antic intimates of death, the gravedigger and Yorick. *Hamlet* is, among other things, an analysis of the role of theatrical modes in mastering our lives; the antic disposition is used with what seems a full intuition of its connection to our apprehensions of death.

* * *

We have gotten to know the Vice largely as a matter of historical research into the origins of Elizabethan drama, and we have been accustomed to think of him in terms of religious idea—the degree to which the persistence of his role indicates the persistence of medieval modes of thought in Renaissance drama. The point has been well taken for the most part, though perhaps we should have been readier to acknowledge that forms may persist while their meanings change. But as a result we are likely to see the Vice in his medieval context largely *as* idea, a figure whose main role is to enforce a theological argument and whose clowning is so much bread or sugar around the pill. The emphasis may easily have been reversed. If we wish to reconstruct the dramatic experience, and hence the real meaning of the Vice and his plays, we would do well to think of his appeal to the audience as corresponding in intensity and centrality to that of the "intruding" *samuna*. Of course these are plays of immensely greater sophistication than those of Orokaiva society. Nevertheless some of the tension and difficulty a modern reader is likely to find missing from the smooth progress of the Moralities may have been supplied or awakened by the way in which the actor of the Vice could compromise the professed piety of the occasion. *Samuna*-like, he could play upon the devout audience's own rebelliousness and fear, perhaps the very fear of theater itself, the fear of subjecting sacred things to impersonation.

Though Falstaff resembles the Vice-*samuna* only in some respects—his approach to the audience is far more ingratiating, his aggression more oblique—still, like Falstaff, the Vice may have won the audience's sympathy in his efforts to take over the play. In *Henry IV*, part of our awareness of the difficulties of government comes from knowing that Falstaff must be gotten off the stage (and, finally, out of Prince Hal's life) if the play is to be satisfactorily concluded. We know that Hal and the play must turn to more serious affairs, yet at the same time we want Falstaff to stay on stage, expand his part, keep clowning (which he often seems to be trying to do, as in the Boar's Head Tavern scenes). Just as Falstaff stirs us up to a kind of rebellious complicity in disrupting the play, so the Vice's obstreperous appeal may have compelled the medieval audience to a more complicated and direct experience of the obstacles to Christian life. In him they could feel the release of demonism, the dangerous excitements of the dance of death. And when the Vice turned his fire on the Devil, what a relief!

The Vice, like the *samuna* and all such violent buffoons, appeals to the audience by helping it carry out an attack on its own respectability—and at the same time it expresses the audience's fear of this force. It isn't hard to see the connection between the Vice-*samuna* and any number of dramatic characters—Père Ubu, say, or the old women in *Lysistrata*. The point they have in common above all is the raffish, persecutory intensity of their attack on our sensibilities.

* * *

Diderot's argument in the *Paradox of the Actor* that the actor works well only when thoroughly detached from the passion he is portraying would have no power, would certainly not have become famous, if it struck anyone as the simple truth. It works as paradox, not recipe. The force of Diderot's position—and of the seemingly endless traditional debate to which it is a contribution—is that there is something uncanny about what an actor does. Clearly the question as to whether the actor should "feel" the emotions he portrays can never be resolved. The question may be answered both ways on the basis of any good actor's performance. Like any artist he is detached from the effect he achieves. At the same time, he is genuinely the subject of an abnormal transformation. It does not quite work to say he "feels" what he is doing— as we feel it; nor that he feels nothing—as we feel nothing. Garrick putting his face through a door and going through a dazzling series of facial changes impressed Diderot because, he tells us, it showed how independent the spectacle was of Garrick's inner state; but this is plainly only part of the story. The faces Garrick made were not impressive in the way a series of masks swiftly fashioned by an expert woodcarver might be. They were impressive because each was a man's living face—the face of a man fully inhabited by Garrick. Diderot's paradox merely heightens our sense of the gap Garrick leaped in his performance.

"Didst thou not say," Diderot apostrophizes Garrick, "that thy playing was astounding only because thou didst constantly exhibit a creature of the imagination which was not thyself?" This is just the point—what makes the actor "astounding" *is* a paradox. Diderot's essay draws its energy from the strangeness of confronting a highly energized man who is and is not himself.

* * *

The mystery and power of drama are captured in the mystery and power of its great emblem, the mask. The mask suggests the double movement of dramatic elation —both escape from self and self-discovery. The wearer of the mask both hides and reveals himself; he takes on the power and license of invisibility, the license of carnival, which is like the license of any invulnerable spirit—the *samuna* indeed behaves like a carnival clown. Every mask—and every dramatic role—has something of the domino's deliberate refusal to specify, a threatening because all-licensing anonymity.

But if we think of the mask alone, without its actor, another quality stands out. Masks were often, perhaps originally, made out of the skins of animals, and indeed the whole skin might be worn by dancers, huntsmen, and other impersonators. Use of human skins for the purpose is not unknown. The mask in all its forms retains a magical cruelty, a ghostliness, a sense of flaying—a face beside itself, austere with the fact of its separation from the body.

Jean-Louis Barrault has described the power of the mask with great sensitivity:

> A mask confers upon a given expression the maximum of intensity together with the impression of absence. The mask expresses at the same time the maximum of life and the maximum of death.

Such strangeness is present in the actor's art whether he wears a mask or not, but the psychology of the mask will help us to understand it. It draws on a very specific and primitive source of fear, sometimes described by psychologists as fear of "the uncanny" and based on a confusion between the animate and the inanimate:

*A, at 1:9, showed great fear of a velvet rabbit which·
was among his Christmas presents. He screamed and
ran away from it; yet I am confident that he had never
had any unpleasant experience with a rabbit or anything resembling it. At 1:2, X showed great fear of a
Teddy bear when it was moved toward her; she turned
away, trembling in every limb; but when it was still she
would pick it up and kiss it. Two German psychologists
report that "a hare mask caused a child of 1:0 to wince
and strike out, one of 1:5 to scream, and one of 1:9 to
cry, but to laugh at the mask when it was taken off by
the experimenter."*

We seem to be born with or to develop very early a sense
of the animate, almost a sixth sense. Like King Lear, that
great baby, we know when one is dead and when one
lives. At eight months, the infant enters a prolonged
phase of his development during which he learns to
discriminate between his mother and strangers. The
distinction between animate and inanimate also first
appears at this stage, and it is accompanied by a fear of
certain inanimate objects:

> *The child, 11 months and 26 days old, looks search-
> ingly at a baby-sized doll, cocks her head as if to look at
> it from a different angle, then looks at the doll straight
> on and considers it. She is unable to come to a decision.
> After a few moments of contemplation the child begins
> to show unpleasure, becomes restless and cries . . .
> Other incidents eventuate in the child's retreating in
> panic, screaming, kicking and beating the doll.*

Of course a child does not fear all inanimate objects.
These observations suggest, however, that any disturbance to a child's ability to distinguish the animate, any
confrontation with something that invites response as
animate but that turns out to be inanimate, or with
something inanimate suddenly animated, shocks his nerv-

ous system deeply. Adults, too, know the sensation. Perhaps, as Freud believed, it confronts us with our buried conviction of the omnipotence of thoughts. Certainly it seems to suit Freud's account of the uncanny; the shock is like that of a ghost, an eruption of menace in our neighborhood that cannot be assigned to any natural cause.

In the case of the eleven-month-old, the psychic development required by Freud's theory would presumably not yet have taken place, but René Spitz has argued persuasively that an inner psychic aggression is similarly responsible for the infant's fright. His rage and terror, Spitz concludes, stem from the absence of the "dialogue" he expects to occur between himself and this apparently animate object; he is shocked by the cutting off of the natural exchange of aggression that runs between all animate beings. The flow of aggression in a theater from actor to actor and between performers and audience is a heightened version of this "primal dialogue." It should be noted further that drama thrives not only on the presence of this dialogue, but on disturbances of it, as in the use of masks with their uncanny freezing of animate expression.

Far more important, the special uncanniness of the mask is actually present in any dramatic role. One reason for this has already been discussed—the role is a disguise for the actor. But more compellingly, every role possesses, to a greater or lesser extent, a rigid, inanimate, mask-like quality. It has been observed, for example, that some famous dramatic characters owe much in their conception to effigies or icons—pageant figures, sacred images, the stuffed giants of carnival. Tamburlaine, for instance, owes much to the Moors and Turks of sixteenth-century street processionals, and is often described by Marlowe in terms that suggest a huge image of a man rather than a man himself. Muriel Bradbrook has used the term "icon" in referring to this type of characterization, and I would say that all dramatic characterization has, in this sense, an iconic aspect. There is something quickly recognizable or familiar in most dramatic parts and always some persisting simplification or abstraction (the old, old king; the faded belle) that remains fixed against its details and surprises. I would also suggest that we can understand the impact of many plays much better if we consider how the iconic element in a role affects our experience of drama. A huge icon may have an uncanny effect for many reasons—its size, the way it is carried, perhaps even its symbolism—but above all it will be uncanny because of its masklike fixity, the inanimate intensity with which it presents the animate, freezing it into the superanimate. To the extent that a dramatic role has such qualities, it allows the actor to take on some of this iconic uncanniness. It is an aid to his command of terrific energies.

* * *

Why does theater make more frequent use of character stereotypes than other arts? The reason usually given is that the playwright needs to make a quick impression on his audience: a character must be graspable at first entrance. There is some truth in this, but there may also be a more fundamental reason, an inherent propriety in stereotypes that goes beyond the question of short attention spans and instant clarity. I would suggest two explanations. First, stereotypes are not so much reductions of the real world as vividly simplified expressions of the actor's power. Like the antic appearance of the Vice, the punitive rigidity of the miser, the good mother's all-embracing sorrow—each forcefully projects some motif in the actor's repertory of emotional aggression. Second, stereotypes are iconic. They heighten the actor's uncanniness. Being a "type" gives him that inanimate freeze which renders his high vitality and animation more terrific.

∗ ∗ ∗

We are now in a position to develop a theory of the heroic role—and by "hero" I will mean simply the principal character or characters in a play. All works of art explore the world. The deep excitement in our experience of any art springs from the way in which the distinctive appeal of the medium makes contact with our interest in other things, the point or edge where that appeal connects with our awareness of the rest of life. So in drama the point of contact is between the appeal of the performing actor and whatever life he may be said to take on, refer to, or evoke. The question for the playwright in any era must be where can acting, where can theater lead his audience in the world it knows or almost knows? For a major part to be effective, it must find a way to take the actor's terrific powers—his ability to be both frightening and sympathetic, hunter and victim, vulnerable and divine—and attach it to a form in which the audience is ready to recognize these powers and give them credence and assent. The icon chosen will have a special bearing on the fears and freedoms of the age in which the play is written, especially on those freedoms that carry with them a powerful charge of fear. It will provide a point of contact for actor and audience, a leading edge for the play's exploration of the world.

PART II

* * *

HERO

AND

PLAY

*   *   *

As acting itself seems provocative, risky, magnetic, so the heroes of drama appeal to us by going to extremes. But every age will have a different sense of where such extremes, such exciting, actor-like transgressions may be found, and of the kind of person likely to commit them. Each age will have its own image of the simultaneously appalling and appealing stance, of the occupation or preoccupation that elevates and exposes, of the power that puts its wielder into jeopardy.

Accordingly, I propose the following formula: the leading role or roles of any play act out some version of a half-allowed, blasphemous, and sacred freedom characteristic of the era in which the play was written. In the enactment, by the very nature of the freedom pursued, the hero risks destruction.

Dramatic action reproduces and extends the process by which the actor assumes his part. Thus it is inevitably connected with the exercise of dangerous freedom—with aggression, escape, exposure, self-assertion beyond normal limits. The dramatic hero is an embodiment of the theatrical enterprise—of its capacity to release and confront the self through the action of a strangely free yet strangely vulnerable person, its powers of binding the community in the evocation and transformation of communal desires and fears. At the same time, any major role explores the relation of theatrical enterprise to the rest of life. It builds on—and in the work of the greatest playwrights alerts us to—the way in which the magnetism and techniques of acting are implicated in the audience's larger awareness of the world.

A culture's leading dramatic roles reflect its attitudes to actors and acting; but even more they reflect its sense of where, outside the theater, terrific energies are likely to appear. The ambivalent energies aroused by theatergoing congregate in the person of the hero, and are released by the blasphemous/sacred freedom he pursues. He is always in some sense an actor who carries his acting to an extreme and is punished for it, or threatened with punishment. In comedy, his extremism is frequently disguised or protected, the punishment displaced, dispelled, or transformed—by methods I shall consider later in this chapter. In non-comic drama, the formula is more nakedly at work. Thus the examples that immediately follow, though drawn from a representative range of periods, will lean toward the tragic side.

* * *

In Greece, where the actor was regarded as a quasi-religious dignitary, fit for the highest embassies of state, free to travel safely even in war, the heroic role permits the audience to see the actor as a quasi-sacred defier of the gods.

The powers that give the Greek hero a status resembling the gods' make him both awesome and vulnerable. He is like a god, but he is also like an actor. The chorus in the *Antigone* sings, in its ode on the achievements of man: "Wonders are many, but none more wondrous than man," and the word we translate as "wondrous" can also mean "strange" or "terrifying" or even "uncanny." The Greek dramatic hero is always *deinos* in this sense—and, as the chorus goes on to tell us, his wonderful, terrible strangeness is reflected in powers of mind and spirit that challenge human limit, his godlike (though not godly) sway over life (but not death). He is described as a great hunter and conqueror in the ode's opening stanza, as a victim and outcast in the last.

The Greek chorus's habitual conservatism—and its tendency to cliché—spring naturally from its awareness of the hero's paradoxical eminence: it is prudent to respect such a man; it is not safe to be him. Bernard Knox's brilliant study, *Oedipus at Thebes*, shows how all of Oedipus's distinctive attributes represent human capacities that an Athenian audience would have recognized as recently expanded, radically controversial, full of exciting promise, characteristically Athenian—and potentially dangerous. It should be noted that Sophocles' final treatment of the Oedipus legend, which brings the hero to Athens, presents his long, horrible punishment by the gods as having made him holier—and more dangerous still.

Oedipus at Colonus begins with the hero wandering by accident into the sacred grove of the Eumenides at Athens, thus repeating the act for which he was originally punished; once more he has found his way to a forbidden spot. The Greek tragic hero is always such a man. Through arrogance or accident, achievement or some native gift, he enters a sacred precinct, lays claim to something divine—and there he makes his stand, eminent and *en prise*. Like the actor entering the sacred circle of Dionysus, or Agamemnon stepping onto the purple carpet, he is a wonder, the center of attention, something like a sacred image, larger than life, marked out for punishment.

* * *

The Elizabethan hero, like the Elizabethan actor, lived (and died) by the freedom to make a place for himself, a freedom that excited and appalled his age. The heroic role of Elizabethan drama typically allows the actor to appear as a masterless plotter, dangerously placeless, the apparent constructor of an action always ultimately larger than he has shaped.

The status of the actor in Elizabethan times was officially and traditionally low. He was considered little better than a vagabond, a threat to public morals, allowed to perform only if he could obtain the livery and protection of a great lord. Yet the most prominent actors of Shakespeare's day were immensely successful, rising to national popularity, eminent respectability, even great wealth. Though—as always—risky, acting offered a man one of the lightning careers of a speculative and chaotic age. Like Petruchio in Padua or Hamlet at Elsinore, the Elizabethan actors were gifted, protean young men thrown on their own resources, exposed and fascinating. It was an era, as C. L. Barber has pointed out, when a ceremonial conception of reality was giving way to an historical one—a naturally fertile moment for drama. It was equally fertile for actors, whose ability to invent and feign ceremony allowed them to rise in power and prestige.

The figure of the man (or woman) thrown on his own resources, free or compelled to invent ceremonies, to improvise a role for himself, runs through all the drama of this period. Think of Tamburlaine or Viola or Simon Eyre. Think, too, of the revenge hero composing his murderous masque, or of the expelled, ceremony-obsessed rulers of

Shakespeare, inventing terrible or transcendent spectacles to play out before a persecuting world—Lear, say, or Richard II, or Cleopatra.

* * *

The half-forbidden freedom of the heroes of French classical tragedy is the freedom to analyze one's passions, to follow the mind in its scrutiny of self, wherever it may lead. There is a tension here with Christian faith, though it is seldom explicit. The scrutiny may seem devout, or profess devotion, or genuinely be devout in impulse—as Pascal's was—but, like his, it has with its first movement already opened infinite spaces like an abyss, beyond the capacity of any devotion to heal. This is the freedom of the vestibule, the blank and flexible anteroom in which the dramas of Corneille and Racine take place. This room, opening on battlefield, bedroom, and council chamber, but functioning as none, is a model for the mind in its perplexed and exalting intercourse with the body. The French actor is supremely the articulator of a mental state, the all-daring hunter of the passion or conviction whose victim his hunt insures him to be.

We have trouble with Racine and Corneille, and we blame it on the alexandrine and its compact diction, or on our unfamiliarity with the *tirade;* but though these are genuine obstacles, the overriding reason, I think, is that we are unable (as translators, actors, and audiences) to grasp the speeches as hunts or pursuits rather than explanations. In English drama, long speeches generally either represent the eruption of powerful feelings or lay out some plan or bewilderment. Looking for the wrong things, we are likely to miss the analytic anguish of French tragedy, its dangerous, steady probing and constant renewal of risk, and instead see its speeches as mere declamation.

Similarly, Corneille's and Racine's heroes may strike us

as oversimplified or too conventional in characterization if we miss the peculiar histrionic impulse by which they are defined. We tend to see them abstractly, as examples of a situation, illustrations of some variety of double bind. Once again, this is because we overlook the distinctive quality of their thrust toward freedom, which actually generates their situation or pushes the situation to its extreme. Here, too, it is helpful to look for the chorus— the audience-like group within the play that elevates and isolates the central actors. In Corneille and Racine we regularly find a passion and a principle of passion which, though it is given relatively conventional expression by the minor characters, is carried to a far more ruthlessly demanding level by the heroes (as with the passion for "honor" in *Le Cid*). The passion is analyzed and the principle pursued—willingly or not—to the point of supreme risk. We are wrong if we take Roderigue and Chimène simply as ideal exponents of a mechanical system of etiquette, young traditionalists in a society governed by fixed codes. *Le Cid* is a play of generational conflict—a conflict that turns on youth's having the presumption to *be*, with a full and insistent self-consciousness, all that the code of their elders *says*. There is no opposition between love and honor in the play—honor, for Roderigue and Chimène, is what makes them worthy of each other's love and of self-love. Their speeches do not set forth a paradox—oh, what a fix I'm in—but press forward their sense of self—this is what I must do, this is where I must lead—a defiant assertion that is also an exploration.

In all the plays it is *awareness* that is the glory and the villain; the bursts of self-definition, for example, that harrow Phèdre's mind, binding her to the past, laying bare her future. In her great dialogue with Hippolyte, the sense of ferocious movement rises from the fact that all her unconscious sexual moves become gallingly conscious to her as she makes them. At the height of her passion, she sees herself as the monster whose blood she has inherited, and begs Hippolyte to kill her—but the very gesture of self-accusation offers him her body. Here is my heart, she says, and wrestles for his sword—pressing upon him both her desire and her revulsion from it. The desire grows more monstrous in the act of being recognized. Omnivorous awareness eats her up as much as devouring love; it is through the power of her modern mind, trapped and lucid in its primitive, desiring body, that Venus cleaves to her with the full force of vengeance.

* * *

We watch Ibsen's hero opening out an inner space amid the press of determinisms. He has the dangerous freedom that comes from knowing or sensing how these determinisms work—how heredity and society shape and warp men's lives—and the willingness to fight against them, especially against conventional opinion. But the opening out reveals the determined trap; the achievement has the exaltation, isolation, and fatality of the mountain peak. Ibsen's heroes have all the energy and monomania, all the desire to change and build, of the great nineteenth-century reformers and profiteers—but their fury to reconstruct is such that they rip away at everything—problems, people, business possibilities—until they touch the void beneath their energy.

There are many plausible explanations for Ibsen's turn at mid-career from epical poetic drama like *Brand* and *Peer Gynt* to the prose "realism" of *A Doll's House* and beyond, and no single explanation is of course sufficient. But an important reason may be that the expansive canvas of the earlier works tended to blur and dilute one of Ibsen's great themes—the operation in man of a radical misery, a deep inhibition of pleasure, and the peculiar forms this misery takes when confronted with the nine-teenth century's characteristic notions of freedom. The society Ibsen depicts is, of course, not a very free one, and it is certainly a society grimly typical of much nineteenth-century middle-class life; but the ideas of freedom which it fears and suppresses—and yet at moments is drawn to or shaken by—are also typical of the age, and their reformist, reconstructive thrust affected the imagination of capitalists and architects, as well as free-thinkers, new women, and rebellious artists. To read through Ibsen's great prose plays is to experience a bleak and bare recurrence, the misery again and again bulking through the fury to reconstruct. Even to sum it up this way is to blur the point—to make abstract and general what in Ibsen is personal and grindingly specific. What we face in each play is a root and harrowing misery rising steadily from the depths and obscure places of a character's perception, from the source of his grandest desires, his deepest impulse to be clear of the past, to change the terms of life—till the misery towers before him and falls invincibly upon him. *A Doll's House*, in this light, seems almost a last evasion, a final touch of hopeful expansive-ness. Nora goes out into a proper world of jobs and affectionate couples, propelled by a desire that seems almost indistinguishable from despair. But someone who knew the later plays might well suspect that the door she exits through opens not on a bracing social struggle—equality for women!—but on Borkman's and Rubek's and Mrs. Alving's fatal, empty mountainside. (Ibsen's moun-tain scenes are great emblems of his ruling vision, where the sense of aspiration and freedom fuses with a certainty of death, unpleasure, failure to fulfill.) And even if we simply consider the last scene of *A Doll's House* by itself, paying careful attention to the theatrical effects intended, the result is bleak and grim. It is, after all, not Nora whom

Ibsen leaves us with, but Helmer in his pathetic uncertainty (a trapped oscillation that points forward to Mrs. Alving's "Yes, yes! No, no!") and the sound of a door slammed shut. Misery, impossible longing, infinite isolation. And in the last plays a further bleakness haunts the characters: always an inhibition to equal—and ruin—any desire. The theme is there in the poetic plays, but it is diluted by the extravagant mise en scène, the romantic scenic variety that was the nineteenth-century theater's own escapist version of the fury to reconstruct. Against the text, the scenic abundance speaks to us of melioration. The change for Ibsen was not simply to "realism," but to a more focused version of the reality he saw.

(The implications of nineteenth-century dramatic spectacle, with its technological impressiveness and frequent exoticism, are worth some study. Consider *Aida*, the archetypal spectacular opera, composed at the insistence of the Khedive of Egypt, who wished to celebrate the completion of the Suez Canal. Verdi's final tableau, a huge cross section of the Temple of Vulcan, shows conqueror and slave trapped and suffering together, suffocating in a little cell enclosed by massive stone blocks, their tomb a monument, like the Canal itself, to a civilization of imperial builders.)

* * *

The contemporary hero can act on the world only by being conceptually outside it. Like an epistemologist or psychiatrist, he knows a secret behind the appearances of the world, and he acts on the world in a way that deprecates its reality, insists on its theatricality. There are many types: the spoof hero or anti-hero, the manipulator, the historical hero as knowledgeable man (as in Shaw or Giraudoux), the saint, and the improviser or metatheatrical hero who openly makes his stand as a self-conscious actor. But their freedom from false appearances is purchased at the risk of meaninglessness; their most authentic acts must question either their own authenticity or the very possibility of meaning in their lives. Small wonder our most widespread fantasy of the actor is of a glamorous *anomie.*

Ibsen seems to be at the root of this phase too, or at least to provide a convenient point from which to trace its history. While his characters never consciously stand outside the world in the sense I mean, their notions of attachment to the world carry a charge of hopelessness, and by the last plays, particularly *John Gabriel Borkman* and *When We Dead Awaken*, the distance between the hero and any possible sphere of activity seems quite unbridgeable. Beginning, perhaps, with Ibsen's characters' painful, frustrated impulse toward "the joy of life," modern drama seems to have drawn increasing nourishment from the circumstance that man has somehow dropped out of his world, can no longer *be* in the world. The situation makes for problems in the invention of action, but it contains exciting possibilities for the actor, since it reinforces his natural strangeness, his threat of attacking us from the ambush of a role. For a dramatic hero, to stand outside the world is to see the world as theater ("Those people are following a script") and thus to gain freedom, a power over others, a charge of histrionic energy such as Shaw's Caesar or Pirandello's Enrico Quattro or Genet's Madame Irma possesses. But how can such energy engage the world? The danger of this freedom is that it excludes its possessor from action in reality, in a reality, that is, corresponding to his own. The world can never receive its saints, at least if they are Shavian ones—world-changing heroes blessed with a consciousness that places them outside the history they create. But it cannot receive Genet's saintly criminals either. For some heroes, like Eliot's mystical psychiatrist,

Reilly, there is the possibility of another reality—if not for him at least for others like the saintly Celia Coplestone whose feet he may set upon the path. For the others, however, there is only a certain freedom of gesture, exposing the realities of an unreal world. A familiar pattern in twentieth-century theater shows this hero, the source of free energy, moving up to attack the borders of the real and being thrown back in some climactic explosion—as in the revolution in *The Balcony*, the failure of Shen Te's masquerade at the end of *The Good Woman of Setzuan*, the climax of most Pirandello plays—and then, if he survives, the hero falls back to his position outside the system.

Many of Brecht's characters vary the process by being inside the system but not of it, and not recognizing but acting out their alienation. The "alienation effects" Brecht sought, both as playwright and director, heighten our sense of a separation between his characters and their world. In performance, we are expected to see Brecht's characters from a distance; the actor is supposed to remind us that he is not the character he plays. One advantage of Brechtian technique is that, by making the audience aware of the distance between the actor and his role, it gives the actor the energy of someone who stands outside the world even though he is playing a character who is simply a victim of the world's processes. Brecht describes his alienation techniques in the language of austerity, of artistic sacrifice to truth, but in practice they give the actor further ammunition for his ambush of reality. If the character does not recognize the contradictions of the system, the play does, and its style allows the actor to participate in the freedom this knowledge provides, a freedom always nicely adjusted to the Brechtian hero's typical drive—to survive. Mother Courage, Shen Te, Mack the Knife, Garga struggle to beat the system at its own game, to master it, to identify with it. Yet they remain its victims. Like most of Brecht's heroes they are actors who struggle to play the part of the system itself, to become a monstrously animated icon of capitalism. What they discover for us is that such action inevitably alienates the person who plays the part. The more they identify the more alienated they become.

Brecht's skill is such—and his account of it at once so helpful and so misleading—that no one seems to have noticed the immense difficulty he regularly overcomes— the problem of making high drama out of banal survival. It is not that without alienation *Mother Courage* would become a "modern Niobe-tragedy," as Brecht claimed to fear—how interesting it would be if such a modern tragedy were possible! But if the vignettes from life in the Thirty Years' War were not presented with the isolation and selection Brecht imposes, Mother Courage would be a miserable grotesque and her play not a tragedy or a comedy but a monotony of pathos and ignorance. Under such circumstances her survival could be dramatically interesting only if she were a monster of cunning—or a Shavian saint. The style of the play resembles the kind of mise en scène Brecht favored as a director: a few superbly realistic details emerging from a starkly theatrical and at times clinical background, like pieces of anatomy in some elegant surgical theater. And so the actor can be both accurate and superhuman, distanced and absorbed; he can excite us both by his ironic commentary on the part and by his depth of identification—without either falsifying the situation through an irrelevant grandeur of performance or slipping into banality. A Shavian Mother Courage would manage to exist entirely outside the world of the Thirty Years' War; Shaw would devise some Utopian mode of communication that would allow her to flourish in it, bend it to her happy will, without being contaminated by it—except perhaps to be saddened by its contamination as St. Joan and Major Barbara are saddened. All the while she would provoke us, taunt us—as, say, Andrew Undershaft does—because we ordinary mortals cannot escape contamination. After his earliest works, Brecht has much of the Shavian lightness. He works for a texture of alienation surprisingly similar to Shaw's, the Dionysiac lightness of an intelligence free of the system it moves through, free of the sick flesh that tugs at Baal and Garga, but he finds a style that allows that texture to be projected through the agency of chief characters who are nevertheless thoroughly contaminated by their world.

In contemporary drama we regularly see the hero drawing power from his conceptual separation from the world, whether the separation is imposed from without by the playwright, as in Brecht, or actually exists in the character's consciousness as in Shaw. At the same time, the hero is threatened and contaminated not only by the world but by the principle of separation itself. In the *Marat/Sade*, Peter Weiss manages to use both kinds of separation, and to suggest an extraordinarily moving type of threat and contamination by playing them off against each other. In his clash with de Sade, Marat has the more dramatically exciting arguments, the more effective place in the action. He and the chorus project an impulse to freedom that we feel ramping to take over the stage, breaking out in every corner of the asylum. But de Sade has it over Marat in that he *is* de Sade. Marat is simply a lunatic playing the part de Sade has written for him. De Sade's presence, however, is felt most powerfully in his detachment. As the author of the play he is isolated, just as he imagines every man to be isolated in the prison of his body. He cannot join the action, which, though it is in one sense merely a charade, nevertheless comes through to us as *the revolution,* the main event of the play. The performance in the asylum at once deprecates the reality of the world and renders its revolutionary drive attractive and terrifying. The revolutionary mob is a bunch of lunatics—but the equation cuts both ways. We take the revolution no less seriously for taking the madmen seriously—but we take it less hopefully. Do not all revolutions take place in a madhouse? Is not the body a madhouse from which we are trying to escape? Can we escape from the madness that makes us desire freedom? Through his choice of setting, Weiss escapes the shallowness of agitprop and writes a play that arouses us to the full sacredness and blasphemy of the revolutionary idea in our time. He plays on our terrible, infuriating suspicion that the world we are dying to change does not exist, that what we are struggling to overthrow is the daily pretense of coherence and meaning whose weight has become too exhausting to be borne.

"When will you learn to take sides?" cries the radical priest Jacques Roux struggling in his straitjacket, in the play's closing moments—and the passionate sympathy he inspires has little to do with propaganda. It is light-years away, for example, from the ending of another play that ends with a revolutionary appeal to the audience, *Waiting for Lefty.* The distance, one might say, is measured by *Waiting for Godot.* Where are we? What has happened? What is to come? Odets' audience knows; Beckett's and Weiss's do not. To whom does Roux shout, and to what end? Can one imagine leaping up at this conclusion to shout, "Strike! Strike!" as the first-nighters at *Lefty* did? Against what? For whom? The rights of madmen? Nothing is changed by the fact that these are *our* rights too, that Jacques Roux cries out with our own deepest longing for freedom and justice. De Sade's laughter at the end, as his play dissolves in riot, both mocks and welcomes revolution. Weiss himself seems to have been exhausted by his effort. His pronouncements since the play give the impression of a man who would happily be something like the early Odets: a writer, that is, of politically "useful" drama, indeed who thinks the *Marat/Sade* is such a play, a political debate with Marat the victor. But the *Marat/ Sade* simply will not allow us *Lefty's*—or anybody's— hopeful confidence in revolutionary desire. Weiss's play is a masterpiece because it releases impartially all the hope and terror the desire holds.

＊　＊　＊

The nineteenth and twentieth centuries do not, of course, divide up quite so neatly as I may seem to suggest. Many kinds of drama have a foot in both camps. One popular variant of the contemporary hero, for example—Willy Loman is an instance—does not actively penetrate and deprecate the appearances of the world, but is simply seen as trapped and suffering in its questionable reality. At the same time, Willy, like most of O'Neill's and Williams' heroes, can be described, without any intent of condescension, as still engaged in the nineteenth-century inner space project. Theirs, however, is more the Strind-bergian version, where the movement toward inner free-dom threatens the very capacity for free human relations it is struggling to establish. Straining for fulfillment, Strindberg's couples turn into monsters. Miss Julie moves us not merely because she fails to be free but also because she *tries*. Less conscious of his situation, Willy, too, strains to be free, gropes toward an extreme. He is a glaringly self-exposed version of the contradictory drives that lie beneath the notion of American success. Even his affability is disturbing—*we* might become that. He is a victim of society, whose commands he has heeded too well, but one of the things society has been saying to him is *be happy, be yourself.*

Hickey in *The Iceman Cometh* behaves like a classic Ibsenite reformer, like Gregers Werle in *The Wild Duck*, busily forcing people to face unpleasant truths about themselves with disastrous results—a confrontation with the void, with a destructive energy at the base of all aspiration, as shattering as anything in Ibsen. But the world Hickey operates on, the pipe-dream world of Harry Hope's saloon, would be more familiar to Pirandello's and Genet's audience than to Ibsen's. Withdrawal and make-believe in *The Wild Duck* are only partial; in O'Neill's play we are given an entire world whose constituent quality is its unreality, its mere theatricality. To really act, responsibly and freely, in this world is not simply tragic, as it is in Ibsen: it is impossible. Larry Slade, who, like Hickey, seems to see the secret of the world and stand outside it, perhaps offers a kind of Ibsenite alternative solution at the end. He is just free enough to intercede—on behalf of death. And so he sends an old friend's son to suicide as an act of commitment and compassion, an irony Johannes Rosmer might have appreciated, but the world O'Neill leaves us with has no mountain peaks, no dawns, no more independent validity than Madame Irma's brothel.

Most critics seem to consider the point of *The Iceman Cometh* to be that men must live by pipe dreams, but this is no more than the play's donnée—we are meant to sense it from the start. The point—the discovery the action makes for us—is that the alternative to unreality is hate. After we discover the murderous, unsatisfiable rage beneath Hickey's reforming zeal and young Parritt's evasions, we return to the reviving festivities at Harry Hope's with a twinge of relief, a shudder of recognition. The pipe dreams return like peace and goodwill. We have seen reality—its truth is in the bullet, the electric chair, the suicide leap—and we have seen enough.

* * *

The Ibsenite hero is so pitted against the grinding social
and biological forces that rule man's life in the world, the
inner space where he must fight for freedom is buried so
deep within him (deeper and deeper, one might say, as
Ibsen's career progresses), that to possess the freedom is
perhaps already to slip out of the world, to lose contact
with life itself. Putting it this way not only connects the
nineteenth-century hero with his successors, but also
points toward Chekhov's place in the process, for certainly his plays present a unique version of the freedom
that comes with slipping out of the world. Chekhov's
heroes are semi-detached; something has pried them
loose. They are bemused by the unattainable. What is
exciting about them is that we share this sense of
unattainableness and respond to the risky freedom of
exploring it—the risk being paralysis, a loss of the joy
of life, of what is natural and blossoming like Russia's
forests or Mme. Ranevsky's orchard.

Chekhov offers a telling example of the need for
remembering the actor when thinking about drama. In
fact we never think of Chekhov in performance without a
powerful and precise sense of the actor's accomplish-
ment—as much, say, as in thinking about *Hamlet* we are
alert to the niceties of interpretation, to acting difficulties
that must be met and overcome. We often forget the
actor, however, in talking about Chekhov's characters—
as if they belonged in one of his short stories. Yet these
characters and our relation to them would be so different
if it weren't for the way they can be performed. And
though each performance belongs to a particular actor,
the possibility for performance is Chekhov's, and it is as
much a part of the play's design as the setting or the plot.

In Chekhov there is a tension between the setting and
the situation. The comfortable solidity of the scene is
always compromised by invisible deterioration. Process

works against action, and the actor makes his familiar social gestures against a dissolving social background. What impresses us about his power is his ability to show the dissolution, the quicksand lurking beneath the conventionally expressive self. Having learned that Chekhov is comic, we are proudly impatient with Stanislavsky for having missed the point, but Chekhov is comic in a very special, paradoxical way. His plays depend, as comedy does, on the vitality of the actors to make pleasurable what would otherwise be painfully awkward—inappropriate speeches, missed connections, *faux pas*, stumbles, childishness—but the vitality itself must be felt not as a festive liberty but as part of a deeper pathos; the stumbles are not pratfalls but an energized, graceful dissolution of purpose.

Beckett does the same with his Didi and Gogo. They are recognizable comic figures, though of a broader comedy —theirs is the slapstick of circus and silent film—but the vital energy of their routines is caught up in and tainted by their situation. Like Chekhov's heroes they are comedians who cannot escape to the protective world of comedy. Their comedy is in the vein of Shakespeare's Feste at the very end of *Twelfth Night*, the unprotected clown with a belly to fill, a body to satisfy, a mind that hurts, and every gate shut against him, singing about the wind and rain after the golden coherent comedy is over. Chekhov fruitlessly kept telling Stanislavsky that *The Cherry Orchard* was a comedy. It is, but what is funny is that what is funny isn't funny.

Everyone in Chekhov resembles Charlotta Ivanovna, the governess in *The Cherry Orchard*, with her card tricks and ventriloquism. Each in his own way attempts a kind of magic, a spiritual mumbo-jumbo, a little number designed to charm or placate or simply elegize reality— the reality of life slipping away, of the dissolving process.

They are sad clowns, redeemed only by being fully felt as people, and not the comic icons they are always threatening to become—failed shamans, whose magic does not work though it has.cost them everything to perform.

Instead of thinking of individual actors or the chief characters in Chekhov's plays we usually think of the ensemble—and this is no accident. What strikes us in a good performance of Chekhov is not only the realistic rendering of the individuals, but the actors' ability to keep in touch with each other. Typical dialogue in Chekhov seems like an interweaving of separate monologues, each composed of irrelevancies; but what gives the dialogue power is not only that all its comments *are* relevant but that it *is* dialogue. All those self-absorbed nonsequiturs are conceived as responses, and the labor of the ensemble must be to make them so. A delicate, painful, blocked, gappy network of contacts, all contriving to miss the world, to let reality slip away—this is what the actors must make us feel. This joint loss of the world and of each other through loss of the world—is the terrible freedom to which Chekhov's heroes measure themselves, only half-unconsciously. Locked out of the utopia of comedy, refused the individual grandeur of tragedy because they cannot touch reality, sympathetically and with bewilderment observing each other's failed or aimless magic, Chekhov's characters seem to dance—a dance of oblique and thwarted contacts—into a utopia of sadness, protected only by the actors' ability to play together.

* * *

Having raised the subject of the special protectedness of the comic world, I want to make two points here about some comic heroes.

1. It is easy to see that comic heroes, especially the ones who take an active role in the plots of their plays, exhibit an appealing freedom, clearly associated with the actor's

—the freedom of disguise, licensed aggression, etc. Further, that the appeal of this freedom comes, in great part, from its being exercised in circumstances that remind us of the restraints of the real world, especially the restraints imposed by real-life *audiences*—social pressure, familial disapproval, and the like. The tricksy servant, with his *samuna*-like impertinence and violence, is a natural invention for getting the maximum comic play out of familiar social situations. For it is his role, usually on behalf of youth and love, to take on those dour, authoritarian, on-stage audiences, and, one way or another, "break them up." Here are the nobleman, the heavy father, the moneybags, the boss, here are the rule-giving leaders of society saying *no*—and against them is Figaro, Scapin, or the servant of Roman comedy, managing through cunning and nerve and energy to get around them, stand them on their ear, put them through their paces, kick them in the pants, make them all say uncle. The pleasure is in the freedom taken, the freedom to attack and get away with it, to change shapes and improve the world—the actor-like audacity of seizing the stage, throwing yourself into your part, making the world not only play to your script but also applaud you for it. Many other heroes of comedy—young lovers, for example, who take the plot into their own hands—share these qualities.

Yet it may seem hard, in many cases, to find a connection between this sort of easily applauded freedom and the blasphemous/sacred liberties of the great noncomic roles. One explanation is this: Comedy frequently makes us feel *as if* such a freedom were being exercised, even when it isn't. Instead of presenting us with characters who go to superhuman extremes, it gives us characters with what in real-life terms would be superhuman luck, but in the world of the play this doesn't seem like luck at all. Where the non-comic hero acquires his compelling power by exercising a freedom his audience recognizes as at least half-forbidden, powerfully and profoundly dangerous, the comic hero often manages to extract a very similar feeling of freedom from some much homelier kind of activity. Thus, a young lover or clever servant, though acting in what is represented to be an ordinary domestic sphere and claiming no more than ordinary virtues, affects the world of his play as if he possessed extraordinary powers; as if, though charmingly or arrogantly everyday, he could fly to the moon or rule the universe. He takes on—through the plot's courtesy—the invulnerability or license of an immortal. Disguise works for him, the harebrained scheme succeeds, the girl's father comes round, the villain goes to pieces. In turn, his extraordinary ability to control, to escape, to anticipate, to put down lends bravery, eminence, a glow of triumph to just those everyday virtues or qualities that the play represents as responsible for his success. Appropriately enough, these are very often extensions or variants of "common sense." Scapin's ingenuity, Figaro's social intelligence, Mirabell's sensibility, Rosalind's clear-headedness, and the plain-speaking every one of them displays—all take on a magical radiance because they apparently account for the freedom with which their possessors operate. (It is not, of course, that characters of this type don't operate under some sort of restraint, that they can't be foiled or fussed or found out. But they do get away with much that it would be very hard for people like them to get away with in ordinary life—and we are made to feel it is not because they are lucky or superhuman, but because they are virtuous and/or smart.)

2. The "hero" of drama, of any kind, is very seldom a model of conduct in any sense, even in the sense that public heroes or the heroes of song and story are. Even if

he is attractive—in the way a normal acquaintance might be—even if he demonstrates what is normally regarded as excellent behavior, there will be something *louche* about him, something extreme and, to a degree, menacing. In comedy, however, the actor-like loucheness of the hero is often disguised by a curious and effective mechanism. Though his on-stage behavior would in real life be considered extreme to the point of danger, we are nonetheless given the *feeling* that the hero is a model of conduct, and this is brought about by a sense of societal approval on stage. We laugh with him, applaud him, as we know the "right" society of the play applauds him (or would applaud him if it only knew). Again certain types seem devised to meet this requirement—the young man as prodigal, for example, whose excesses can be indulged with our approval, felt as normal and quite compatible with ordinary "niceness." Comic heroes are generally much further from being models of conduct than their tragic counterparts, but they are protected by being treated as models—or at least as tolerably decent—in a special world.

(An interesting variation on this moral sleight-of-hand may be found in the verbal technique of *The Importance of Being Earnest*. Here a quite bogus tone of good manners, adopted by all the characters, is miraculously accepted as genuine. In social intercourse, the characters are by real-life standards monsters, absolutely in earnest about only one thing—their appetites. Algy, Jack, Cecily, and Gwendolen, like the privileged young idlers they are, draw ruthlessly upon their wealth and status to get their way; but unlike their real-life counterparts, they express themselves directly; they always say what they mean. When they don't like something, they heap contempt upon it; when they want something, they ask for it directly and give a plain reason for gulping it down. [In this, as in so much else, they are like children. The play has all the innocent savagery of a nursery romp in which the nannies have magically shrunk and the fathers vanished entirely.] But—and this is the point of the technique—it doesn't *sound* as if they were saying what they meant. It sounds like a supreme form of polite repartee, idly but perfectly phrased. Indeed their speech has all the self-satisfied music of Victorian high moral tone. Though they express their desires nakedly, it is always as if from the heights of rectitude. Here we come upon both the technical principle and the dramatic function of the play's verbal style. The brilliant humor of the dialogue depends very much on the truths of appetite being uttered with all the elegance of polite lies.)

*   *   *

The ideas I have been exploring in this chapter provide clues to the life and interest of many difficult dramatic texts. They may in fact prove especially useful where the secret of a text's dramatic life and interest seems especially remote from our theatrical experience. Take, for example, a persistent difficulty one meets in the interpretation of medieval drama. In spite of much excellent recent scholarship, the modern reader is still likely to find that the histrionic force of much of this drama eludes him. By histrionic force I mean the whole felt appeal of the plays as acted, the precise texture and purport of the dramatic excitement they are designed to sustain. It is much easier to imagine the charged and shaping interplay between Sophocles' actors and their Athenian audience than that between the good amateurs of the York guilds and the audience at the festival of Corpus Christi, who watched them perform their vast cycle of plays, taking days to complete and stretching from the Creation and the Fall of Lucifer to the Last Judgment. Without a sense of the plays' actual dramatic interest, our sense of their meaning and quality must remain general and incomplete. Our mental and chronological distance from this drama is vast indeed, and no technique can bring us anything like certainty. Still, I would like to risk here a tentative interpretation of the histrionic force of the great English cycles of the fourteenth and fifteenth centuries. It is based on two ideas developed in this chapter: the special protectedness of the comic world, and the blasphemous/sacred freedom associated with acting.

The first thing to observe is that the *distance between actor and character* is greater in these plays than in any other phase of Western drama. In medieval performance, the actor in the cycles was *one of us*—a local amateur most of the time—while the character was *one of them*—usually a sacred personage, at least a figure in sacred history. This distance was reinforced by a powerful awareness of the presumption involved in an actor's undertaking such roles at all. There was indeed a widely recognized risk of blasphemy in playing these sacred figures, and it must have been taken seriously not only by the clerical writers who attacked the drama, but by the audiences and actors themselves. In every dramatic version we have of the Fall, Lucifer is punished for *playing God,* for attempting (literally) to sit in God's throne. So the cycles normally began with an impressive reminder of the potential blasphemy of acting.

As V. A. Kolve has pointed out in his path-breaking book, *The Play Called Corpus Christi*, this problem is met by the insistence, throughout the cycles, that what is happening on stage is a kind of play, a game, a "jest," a "jape," a "bourd." The notion of the drama as play and game thus constitutes a kind of protection for the actor. Now, there is a parallel between this protection for the actor and the central subject of the cycles—the larger protection for all mankind offered by the Christian dispensation. We feel it, for example, in the treatment of the soldiers who torture Christ in the Crucifixion episodes. Christ, of course, forgives them, "For they know not what they do"; but the dramatic justification for Christ's assertion seems to be found, in all the cycles, in having the torturers treat their efforts as a game or a series of games, in which they are so absorbed that they scarcely focus on the identity of their victim. Their blasphemy may be forgiven because it is committed in play.

I believe that we are meant to be aware of a dramatic thrust, underlying all the cycles, to convert the potentially blasphemous play of the actors into an act of grace, and thus to dramatize the power and glory of the Christian dispensation. Man is forgiven for his presumption in playing the role of God and in making light of serious things, and so his play is transformed by the grace of God into celebration. The celebration that the play constitutes thus becomes a way of closing the gap that exists between the eternal characters and the amateur actors— a process that echoes the miracle of the Incarnation itself, that closes the gap once and for all between human and divine.

The process is felt with exemplary force and clarity in the *Second Shepherds' Play* of the Towneley cycle, especially in the interplay between its sacred subject and secular subplot. In the course of the main action the Shepherds learn of the Nativity and go to the manger to worship the Child. In the subplot, they suspect that one of their number, the deceitful Mak, has stolen a sheep; he attempts to pass the animal off as his new-born child, but the shepherds discover the imposture and punish him. The parallelism of the two plots has often been noticed, but even more interesting is the way in which their juxtaposition embodies the whole effort of the cycle to transform the activity of the actors into the proper celebration of Christ.

We see the Shepherds first as worn, embittered men— not very different from Mak. At the end they resemble gentle children, not entirely divorced from the Child they honor. They begin by complaining of the cold and of the oppression and exploitation they suffer; they end in joy, presenting naïve gifts (a bunch of cherries, a tennis ball) to the Child, and singing loudly. A current of racy, colloquial anachronism—typical of the cycles, though here unusually fine—animates their dialogue throughout. Its effect is to heighten our sense of the distance, and yet the contact, between the amateur local actors and the lofty, eternal event which they enact.

The blasphemous potential of acting is emphasized in the person of Mak, who is presented from the start as an actor. Dressed in a cloak he has stolen, he acts as if he didn't know the Shepherds, pretends to be the King's messenger, at some point adopts a phony south England accent. Later, his wife suggests the "bourd" of pretending the sheep is their child, and she gives a noisy and convincing imitation of a woman in labor, while he vigorously plays the attentive father. Like the stage version of the Nativity we are about to witness, Mak's little drama is not the real thing but an impersonation. It is a criminal substitution of animal for human. Is not the actors' imitation, not only of the Nativity but of all sacred history, an at least equally criminal substitution of human for divine?

We are never far, however, from the opposing notion: that the play of the actors can be touched with grace, and thus constitute not blasphemy but true worship. This is heightened by the behavior of the Shepherds throughout, particularly in their encounters with the infant Christ and the Angel. They are at their most playful and child-like here—not the least, one imagines, as we watch them learning to sing a hymn to the Child. There is much singing in the play (including a loud, out-of-tune lullaby from Mak during the false Nativity), and when the Shepherds hear the Angel sing, they comment on his technique and try to imitate him. One can only guess here, but it is likely that their attempts to master this new song (perhaps awkward at first, then finally successful) were meant to form a significant part of the pleasure of the play. Their efforts would certainly have provided a fine emblem for the efforts of the Towneley actors to properly celebrate their subject.

The *Second Shepherds' Play* succeeds by firmly locating the divine event in a real human landscape, whose wintry bleakness and harsh realism serve to underline the transforming force and value of the Christian dispensation—a transformation of the humblest by direct impingement of the highest. The Christian view is thus "comic" not only in the traditional sense—seeing life as a progression from sorrow to joy, from earth to heaven—but in the sense that it finds natural expression in a type of protectedness we have seen to be characteristic of much comedy. Not only the *Second Shepherds' Play*, but the cycle dramas as a whole, present a world that, by divine intervention, has become charged with that very possibility for enhancing the ordinary which comic action so often provides. It is a world in which the ordinary capacities of humble men easily take on a superhuman power—as if the humbleness, the ordinary virtue, were itself the power. Thus, throughout these plays, a medieval audience would find a sustaining current of dramatic interest generated by the interaction between a protected play-world and the exciting and risky freedom of local actors assuming roles from sacred history.

* * *

When a theater audience loses interest we say that the illusion fails. But what does it mean that the illusion fails? That reality has succeeded? No, we're aware that in the theater when illusion fails, reality, too, in some sense has failed. The idea of a protected world clearly applies to all kinds of drama, tragedy as well as comedy. Our question, then, has to do with what really is happening when we feel that this protection is being successfully maintained through time, with how the play itself keeps the performer-audience relation alive in its full evocativeness. In short we need a workable notion of dramatic interest, of the way in which what we call the illusion is sustained so that we remain subject to its spell.

Let me start with a passage from Piaget about illusion in children's games. The emphasis is mine:

> *Deliberate illusion . . . is merely the child's refusal to allow the world of adults or of ordinary reality to interfere with play, so as to engage a private reality of his own. But this reality is believed in spontaneously, without effort, merely because it is the universe of the ego, and* the function of play is to protect this universe against forced accommodation to ordinary reality.

This is immensely suggestive. So many familiar counters of aesthetic theory—"illusion," "interest," "suspension of disbelief"—seem to be attempts to evoke the flow of unbroken ego-satisfaction, the non-disruption of our pleased attention to a work of art. Just as Piaget distinguishes between the child's play and the universe of his ego, which his play protects, we can make a distinction between the universe of the work of art as we experience it and its "play"—what we ordinarily think of as the work's "design," "style," "form." These will have the primary function of protecting the universe of the work

from disruption by a principle that can fairly be connected with "reality." Piaget goes on, it is true, to
distinguish children's play from drama and poetry with
their "consciousness of make-believe," but the two- to
four-year-old has a consciousness of make-believe too,
and while it may differ from an adult's in some respects, it
clearly allows for a "consciousness of reality" which is
not unlike our own in the presence of drama. Piaget says
the child "does not consider whether his ludic symbols
are real or not. He is aware in a sense they are not so for
others, and makes no serious attempt to persuade the
adult they are." Actors, of course, may be said to try to
persuade their audiences that their actions or emotions or
the props they wield are "real," but the standard of
realism invoked is radically different from that used to
judge actions, emotions, and objects in "real life." It has
to do with maintaining a relation to the outside world,
keeping the outside world under control, as it were, but
not with passing muster as part of the outside world.
Though we are aware as perhaps—only perhaps—the
child is not, that the symbols of art are not real for us, it is
still true that as we watch the play, to the extent that it is
successful, *we do not consider whether the symbols are
real.* We do not judge them by standards that refer
directly to the outside world, but by standards established
within the work itself. The play protects the ego-universe.
But the ego-universe is specifically filled and constituted
by the content of the play. If we think of the design of a
play (and this can include any of its definable elements—
language, rhythms, disposition of the scene, themes,
characters, plot) as protecting its satisfactions, we have
made a start toward extending our theory of performance
to a poetics of the dramatic text.

* * *

Piaget is describing a process that takes place in the mind of a single individual who is both performer and audience. His description needs to be modified to account for the audience-performer relation. Here we will be helped by some observations made by Donald Kaplan, who draws a parallel between the psychoanalytic notion of "transitional objects" and the experience of watching actors in a play. Taken in conjunction with Piaget's, his insight is very helpful.

Kaplan sees the script as a type of transitional object, like the child's security blanket—a piece of external reality that is treated as if it were purely internal, and not differentiated from self. For the child, the blanket is a little bit of the world that is also a little bit of himself. For the actor, the script is both something he must follow and a current of emotions and expressions he can call his own. The difference, of course, is that the script is a *shared* transitional object. Objects like the security blanket are called transitional because they appear during a phase when the child is learning to differentiate the external world from himself; by bridging the two realms they help make the accommodation less threatening. Translating this into Piaget's terms, we could say that the transitional object protects the child's ego-universe. Kaplan, too, sees that the script is protective—of a world held in common by actor and audience:

> The script regulates . . . the possibilities of too great or too little illusion in the performer-audience relationship by creating a shared realm between the performer and audience in which the very formulation of questions of illusion is not made.

Imagine yourself playing Hamlet and, after a few minutes, suddenly forgetting the lines. The collapse and fear you feel come from and represent the loss of a protection that has allowed you to carry on your play, to develop and extend it without any break that would let the real world enter—or rather it has let the real world in, other actors, the props and situations on stage, the crowd staring at you, but only by building them into your play, making them part of your ego-universe. The script has built the outside world into your play. And for the audience, though the risk has not been so great, the process has been similar. (The risk has been similar too. Examine your reactions, as a member of the audience, when a good actor in an interesting play muffs his lines badly. The dismay is not only on his behalf. Even more striking, think of what you feel when someone in the theater disrupts the performance. The shock, the upset we experience at such moments is out of all proportion to the "real" threat involved. The security blanket has been yanked from our hands.)

The state of attention nurtured by the script is clearly very similar to that which Piaget posits for the child at play. The drama protects actor and audience from what Piaget would call "forced accommodations to reality." Once more we find a close parallel between children's play, acting, and a primitive sense of the pressure of otherness—a pressure that may not only be felt as threatening from the outside, but as thrusting out from within, the uncontrolled aggressions and apprehensions with which we have daily to cope. Through the script, the actor can work to take over these threatening forces and convert them into his freedom—into a countering, mastering energy, an elated sustaining tension, a "primal dialogue," on which audiences thrive.

The kind of violent demonstration of dislike we associate with the theater—the audience breaking up the play—resembles, as Kaplan himself points out, the "snake pit" phenomenon of the insane asylum, where unshared fantasies break in upon one another. The sudden rupture of the shared fantasy leads to similar outbreaks of aggression by the audience. But we can now add a further reason for the rage: the sudden loss of ego-protection as the design fails to keep our sense of ordinary reality at bay.

Since the transitional object, the script, protects the universe of performance, and since the script helps create this universe as well as protect it, we may describe any dramatic text, in an elementary fashion, as coordinating three elements: the energies of the actor, an "icon" or mask, and the "world" of the play. This last is in part a purely invented world given by the words of the script and the gestures of the actor, but it also inevitably bears relation to the ordinary world and to the fantasy world or ego-universe of the audience. It is a protected version of our world—protected not from the appearances of the ordinary world, or from our recollections of it, but from the demands that world makes upon us.

* * *

We find here the true status of the "desert" of realism Eliot misjudged. Drama is always poised between the real and the conventional, and the presence of the two, each imposing different conditions, is part of the most elementary dramatic excitement. The pure or "consistent" convention, as Eliot called it, is impossible in drama, would be fatal if possible, because it would suppress entirely the living presence of the actor. Theater is here and now, difficulty being overcome before our eyes; the performer is using not only his whole body but his whole being—we are supposed to attend to everything about him. Everything that we can see or feel him doing is legitimately part of the performance he is creating, and any of it can make a difference to the play. That glass has to be lifted and drunk from *now;* even the most hieratic gesture of the

Noh must be executed by this man *here* at this moment, lifting that hand which is his own hand but also the hand of the character. . . . The fact that the actor is, inescapably, alive means that there is always extra reality thrusting to break into the convention, and this gives added intensity to our natural awareness of unaccommodated reality thrusting and threatening to break into the play-world in which we are absorbed. We like to see the real in the theater, but it threatens the play; we like to see it *because* it threatens. Are those real tears Hamlet is weeping? Well and good. And do they seem to draw on an emotion the actor is experiencing here and now? Even better. Yet the actor by indulging his private sorrow—or too directly appealing to our own—may ruin everything. Real tigers make the circus interesting. They are less real if they are barred from all contact with us, but we cease to be an audience—our play-time is over—if they are let loose. Hence the lion-tamer. There is a cage for protection, but someone is inside the cage. And if he were able to control the animals with bare hands—if he didn't need whip, gun, chair—so much the better. But if they bite off even a single finger, the show is over.

∗ ∗ ∗

Imitation in the most general sense—you lift your arm and baby lifts his arm—is what Piaget calls an "adaptive" act. It submits the ego to the requirements of an external world. Play, as Piaget distinguishes it from imitation, is "assimilative." It generates bodily activity without submission, expanding the ego-world without stress from the outside. It is characteristically free of the outside world, that is to say, it carries the physical implications we later associate with the word "freedom." In its simplest form, assimilation is the pure play of the body: baby lifts his arm and waves it around his head. At the level of infant behavior and for the purposes of scientific description,

Piaget's distinction is workable and significant. Fully scrutinized, however, his two terms cannot be kept apart any more than the notion of freedom can be kept simple and clear. And indeed Piaget as an observer seems fully aware of their practical interrelation. As the child grows, his play becomes an increasingly explicit method of relating to the world; it becomes mimetic. Piaget places great emphasis on what he calls "symbolic play." In its simplest form, this is the substitution, in play, of one object for another. A child pushes a box, pretending it is a car. Brilliantly, Piaget observes that this is a way of learning to think, learning to move the objects in the real world as part of the play of the mind, moving them as later he will move ideas and images. The symbolization quickly becomes complex, and its use as a means of handling the stress of external reality expands rapidly toward the full subtlety of human thought and imagination. It quickly leads children to the compensations of play-acting and later to the eager taxonomy of games.

The play-acting tendency is established, however, well before the appetite for games with rules assumes its sway:

> At 3:11 (21) she was impressed by the sight of a dead duck which had been plucked and put on the kitchen table. The next day I found J. lying motionless on the sofa in my study, her arms pressed against her body and her legs bent: "What are you doing, J?—Have you a pain?—Are you ill?—No, I'm the dead duck."

The kind of activity described here is not quite acting. It is an example of an early level of symbolic play in which the child's body is substituted for the duck's. But the movement is as much toward acting as it is toward thought— this is clearly a way of learning to think about death. It is certainly adaptive: the duck's disturbing condition is submitted to; but it is also assimilative. There is freedom and satisfaction in the act. And in true acting we can likewise see the crossing of play and imitation in Piaget's sense of the terms. The purely mimetic aspect of the art can be described as adaptive—the actor submits himself to someone else's gait—but this is accompanied by a play element in which mastery is self-delighting as well as self-disciplining. This is why it is fatal to discuss acting as if it were merely mimetic; it ignores a quality that is fundamental to dramatic art. What I have called the "terrific" side of acting flows from the process of assimilation. Acting is a way of learning to think with the body. It is a way of learning through the body to be free of all that limits or threatens the body, to give the body the freedom of the mind—and to free the audience's mind through its response to the actors' freedom.

* * *

It is the play element, then, the "assimilative" side of acting, that dramatic theory has failed to take into account. Discussions of comedy, in particular, often go astray by overlooking the role that the actor's power over his body plays in comic effect. Writing about Falstaff once, I distinguished Falstaff's appeal from the very different comedy of Francis, the hapless robot-like butt of the tavern scene, by calling Francis's the comedy of mechanism and Falstaff's the comedy of irrepressibility. The terms stand for two familiar elements in comedy—and in the theory of comedy. Comedy of mechanism recalls Bergson, and it fits many comic effects well, but I see now that when we think about comic performance we are likely to find it a dangerous term. For in performance —at least when the performance is good—all comedy is the comedy of irrepressibility. Some comic effects may derive from the reduction of the human to the status of the automaton, but the comic actor is never an automaton. When Jacques Tati, hurriedly climbing the stairs at a railway station, catches his umbrella handle in an iron grating and is suddenly jerked backwards, the character he is playing has for an instant become a puppet propelled by the world's lifeless mechanism, but in that instant Tati is himself most characteristically alive. For it is neither the umbrella, the grating, nor the laws of motion that are propelling Tati; it is Tati himself. That lunatic change of direction imitates the body suddenly helpless before the forces it cannot control—but it is expressive of immense ebullient control and of immense geniality of spirit. And Tati makes of the movement (and of the whole sequence of movements of which the jerk backwards is a part) something elegant, vital, madly rhythmic, something funny. It is the irrepressible Tati. We pay to see Tati catch his umbrella in the grating, not someone accidentally doing so. A man slipping on a banana peel may make some bystanders laugh—a nasty lot they would be—but it is not comedy. Chaplin slipping on a banana peel is. For in the very act by which the ordinary spirit is degraded, the clown's is triumphant. Like the shaman or the primal actor dressed up in animal skins, he seizes control of the otherness which threatens to destroy him and his community. Every comic gesture is a little resurrection.

* * *

Acting transforms adaptation into assimilation as the actor's special kind of mimesis transforms the terror of what is outside the actor into the terrificness of his performance. Script and performance work together to sustain this crossing of play and imitation in the experience of the audience. The playwright aims to encourage the actor to bring his energies to bear in a way that will seem to matter. But the criterion here is nothing so simple or narrow as the notion of "relevance"; the idea that dramatic interest is a sign of sustained ego protection provides a more accurate standard. To borrow a word from Arnold, drama needn't be about the world as we know it, but it must be *adequate* to it. The play of the actor must stand up in relation to the outside world—to which we are constantly adapting, constantly forced to adapt, constantly aware we must adapt, and against whose stresses the ghostly impulse to autonomy beats in fear and exaltation. If this awareness of the "real" world—that is, of the variety of adaptations likely to be demanded from us—is not met by the opportunities for dramatic assimilation, the play-universe (which by now corresponds more or less to part of our ego-universe) will cease to be protected.

* * *

Tragedy seems actually to invite the world into the work in its most threatening form—in a form precisely designed to risk the destruction of the ego-universe the work maintains. It is just the things we have to shut out of our minds to keep from going crazy, just the explicit threats we might ordinarily expect entertainment to fend off, that tragedy lets in. Its art, of course, lies not in simply letting them in, but in letting them in without smashing the work to pieces. The greatest drama will be the one which risks the greatest danger of accommodation to reality and yet maintains the universe of satisfactions unbroken, or at least undestroyed. The blinding of Gloucester asserts the size of *King Lear*'s achievement by forcing the sense of risk almost unbearably upon us. Shakespeare characteristically makes even the fact of the risk—and our reaction to it—part of the dramatic meaning of the scene. *Lear* is not only about human pain but about the ways in which we try to cope with it, including avoidance. The blinding of Gloucester makes us try to avoid the pain and then tortures us by not letting us get away. We may try to generalize the experience—"Oh, his eyes are being put out"—so Shakespeare particularizes—first one eye is put out, then there is a pause . . . we are urged to note the results—and only then does Cornwall go after the other eye. Or we may react by closing *our* eyes; so Shakespeare provides a running narrative that is as horribly particular as the visible scene—climaxing with a hideous verbal closeup of the second eye:

> *Out, out vile jelly,*
> *Where is thy luster now?*

The method of *King Lear* is to lead us regularly up to a point that is felt to be "the worst," to make us feel we have seen as much as the play is shaped to take of mental and physical suffering, and then to show us something that is worse still. The play's greatness lies in its earning its way through suffering—achieving a sense of discovery and completeness that grows with every shock. The protection seems to fend off nothing but to invite all the pain we know into our play.

* * *

A word about subtext. Theater is not simply a place of disguise, but of men disguising. So, for a play to be interesting, the disguises must always be under stress or in change. In the work of any competent playwright or actor, disguise is constantly being assumed and stripped away, constantly growing and transforming. Acting (and this is one difference between professional and amateur actors, though not every professional pays enough attention to it) is not a matter of assuming a fixed role but of showing how the character *acts*—that is, how he moves in and out of his repertory of roles; how he changes his disguise to meet every moment of the play, responding to changes in his situation and in the characters around him, revealing one thing and hiding another. Here again, acting itself is always in some sense the subject of the play.

I can't think of better advice for a young actor than to remember that in any part he plays he must be changing masks from moment to moment. The life of any performance may be measured by the rate of change, and will depend on the actor's ability to spot a shift in the character's on-stage audience or in the character's perception of his audience (on-stage or off) or in the role he is playing for them. And the actor's analysis of character will always benefit from thinking of the character as an actor—how does he read his audience? what is his repertory? what is the principle by which he changes masks?

Speech in particular, because of its mobility, its density of impressions, should always be thought of as a disguise —a disguise that slips, reveals, changes, strains to be adequate, strains even to be true or transparent to what it describes, breaks away, breaks down, stiffens, must be bolstered up. It is the fastest-changing mask of all. Thus there is always a subtext, a movement against or away from the "literal" statement of the speech. It is a means, provided by the playwright, by which the actor may keep in touch with the acts his character is putting on, or that the pressures of life—outer and inner—are making him put on.

Sometimes the masks are simultaneously present—one peeping out from behind the other, the action or dialogue a spotlight quickly picking them out in turn. In any good scene or speech, we can look for a multiplicity of masks, a multiplicity of intentions that spring from a multiplicity of performances by the character for various audiences or one audience variously conceived. Even in the messenger speeches of Greek tragedy we have at least four actions going on at once, which represent four kinds of performance and thus four masks for the messenger: (1) the narrative—the messenger as transparent reporter; (2) the re-enactment—the messenger responding to the physical movement of the scene he describes; (3) the recollection —the messenger struggling with the pathos he has experienced; (4) the performance—the messenger presenting himself to his on-stage audience. This is what makes such speeches hard for the playwright, and what makes them effective in the theater. Anyone who tries to write a messenger's speech that will *play,* that will keep the actor alive in his art for its entire length, or any actor who tries to deliver, say, the messenger's speech in *Hippolytus* as just one kind of performance, will quickly see the truth of this.

* * *

Etonne-moi, said Diaghilev with the instinct of a man of the theater. For theatrical excitement has an affinity with the shocking. One kind of shock, of course, destroys the play, and—as we've seen—all ruptures of the protective design, all failures of art in the theater—even boredom— must be shocking. The sense of outrage and the sense of pleasure are perhaps more closely related in theater—the line between them narrower—than in other arts. A fantasy aroused carries with it the awareness of the stress it protects against or adapts to, and if we are outraged in the theater when the action fails to integrate or protect our aroused fantasies, we feel pleasure when the fantasy is allowed full exercise, when we can ride with it and feel its fears at play in the living bodies of the actors. Often the force of this excitement is felt as the risk of shock— nearly too much, adaptation to our fears pressing fiercely against assimilation, as in the putting out of Gloucester's eyes or perhaps that legendary first appearance of Aeschylus's Furies to the shocked Athenian audience, when pregnant women were so frightened they miscarried. But this, I would judge, is only an extreme version of the near disturbance, the nearly shocking release, present in any great play. In the greatest drama, the excitement is felt, above all, as an opening out of our world—and it springs from the appearance of a figure or a freedom in whose enactment the mixture of so much that is fearful and exalting is possible.

* * *

The affinity with the shocking may help account for the sudden richness and relative instability of the great phases of dramatic history. Two things, at least, seem to happen together at such moments, which allow for a sense of dangerous freedom exercised satisfyingly on stage. A certain class of heroes is discovered, and, even more important, a means is found to place them in a resonant dramatic world. In English drama, to concentrate on a single example, the sudden achievement from about 1588 on would seem to be the creation of heroes—Tamburlaine, Hieronimo, and then the tremendous line—and of course they are of unprecedented size and power. But the deeper and crucial achievement is the creation of heroes-in-a-world, the establishment of an actor in a role which takes on a recognizable and consistent place in an invented world that bears an exciting correspondence to the audience's own. The analogy of perspective is attractive. Before 1588 we find the theater already catering to many of the appetites that the great Elizabethan and Jacobean plays were to satisfy, but as yet only separately, in fragmentary fashion. The audience wanted and got exoticism, violence, pictures of the great world, the problems and personalities of government. The actors in *Cambises*, say, could show various interesting activities in a loosely representative frame. Here was an up, there was a down. Here was a spectacular murder, there a piece of lechery. Bits of disconnected intrigue materialized and vanished. Cambises performed one or two just acts, a number of wicked ones, and then died suddenly. A great deal happened, but the sequence and emphasis were almost entirely arbitrary. There was no coherent sense of what was at stake in Cambises' world, what it took to hold it together or shake it, how one figure or action weighed against another. The audience saw kings and princes doing lots of exotic, violent, high and mighty things, but the "Persia" in which they claimed to do them was only a platform. With the work of Kyd and especially Marlowe, however, everything the actors could do took effect on a stage and in an imagined world that had the recognizable shaping presence of the world the audience knew. The actions were interconnected; every event was proportioned by a plan. The audience was able to measure the hero's achievements on a scale in his world that clearly corresponded to the scale by which men and events were measured in its own. Above all, the stage-world was consistent and complete. The frame had its own laws of motion and coherence, and all action within the frame obeyed the law. Compared to this achievement, the development of the well-made play in the nineteenth century represented simply a change in the law—the Elizabethan contribution was the coherence and autonomy of the law itself.

That the physical world has its own laws and that these are of great interest—this aspect of the "new philosophy" had its counterpart not only in the structure of plays but in the new conception of the dramatic hero. Like the new actors he was a man whose invented ceremony challenged all ceremony, who stood out against the invariant social frame with a frightening and alluring mobility. To place him firmly in the perspective of the Renaissance world and the Renaissance theater was to make him an actor in the world, a genuine agent whose behavior made itself felt according to the coherent physics of that world.

Action in this new world—the coherent world represented by the theater—revealed and was governed by a physics. The performance revealed and was governed by a plot. Every Elizabethan dramatic hero is a plotter—someone who tries to take charge of the laws by which things move and change in his world—or the fighting victim of a plot. That crucial Elizabethan creation, the revenger, is above all things a maker of plots. If the audience responded to him because he helped intensify their feelings about the man who played him, his actions were remarkably like those of the man who wrote his part. The revenge hero is a composer of tragedies whose denouements invariably take place before an audience.

"Who cannot be crushed with a plot?" asks Parolles, Shakespeare's wordy comic butt in *All's Well*; this is the comic question. The heroes of comedy are protected either from or by the plot; the butts are sacrificed to it. Parolles' is the tragic question, too; only, in tragedy, it is not rhetorical. "Simply the thing I am shall make me live," says Parolles as he limps off, scroungy to the last; but this line, with its surprising starkness, looks forward to the later tragedies—*Lear, Macbeth, Coriolanus*—and their searching examination of the self. What remains after the plot has crushed you, or what it is that cannot be crushed—this is what English tragedy defines.

* * *

No one imagines that Seneca + Machiavelli + A + B . . . = Revenge Genre. An influence is not a banker; most studies of literary influence seem modeled on the question, where did he get his money from? But a *readiness* for a certain kind of expression can attach itself to a particular source, taking over whatever pertinence or usefulness it has. It was exactly for what, in the imagination of the age, they already represented that Seneca and Machiavelli were invoked. The appetite which seized on the plays of Seneca and the appetite which was reflected in the interest in Machiavellianism were elements of a larger appetite for dramatic expression, a need—and a readiness—to reconceive the world in dramatic terms, to turn actors loose in a new kind of theater, to make their freedom new and newly significant to the audience—all of which found an outlet in revenge drama.

Basically, the appetite for both Seneca and Machiavelli was an appetite for action, or rather for a relation of performance to action, which seems to parallel the relation already discussed in this chapter, of the actor to his world. The Senecan contribution was a rhetoric that made suffering action, or rather pushed suffering toward dramatic action by making it aggression. It allowed psychic states to come thrusting out at the audience. The expansion, intensification, and elaboration typical of Senecan rhetoric allows the audience to be caught up in that familiar Elizabethan grip of half-insane agitation, of an ego enlarging itself through and beyond the largest available objects of desire or destructive will. Its related achievement is to connect this intensity to a large world by sweep of reference, that geographical and cosmological reach which is not exclusively Senecan but can only be used effectively in stage speech when it can be attached to the thrust of an actor's personality, as it is in Seneca—and is not in Virgil and Ovid. Once again, what makes Seneca important in the history of English drama is not his imagery or his grisly paraphernalia; it is the histrionic originality of his verse. To argue that Kyd, in *The Spanish Tragedy*, is more indebted to Virgil than to Seneca because the geography, scenery, and inhabitants of his Hell are borrowed from the *Aeneid*, to point out that Seneca's Tantalus dwells, as Kyd's Don Andrea does not, on the horror suffered in Hell is to miss the crucial point—that it is exactly Seneca's feeling for "horrors" as a source of dramatic energy, for description as a vehicle for powerful histrionic emotion, that Kyd has seized on with an opportunism that makes him one of the seminal figures in English drama.

It is only when revenge is hit upon as the source for a complete play that the dramatic possibilities of Seneca's rhetoric (scarcely exploited in his own plays) are released on the stage. For the revenger is a character to whom all the rhetorical intensities of the Senecan tradition can be attached. Haunted by his complex, burdensome, and galling task, the revenger carries with him a suffering always near to the surface, always pressing toward enactment, focusing in hate, bursting out in rage, but never—till the climax—capable of being fully released. It was quickly discovered that a variety of heroes could use the new instrument—could have a strong, shaping, varied emotional current vividly running through them throughout a play; but they all owed something to their revenge forebears, or, more precisely, to the figure of whom the revenger is but the most striking example, the Machiavellian hero. As Seneca's rhetoric allowed feeling to come thrusting out in performable aggression, so the Machiavellian interest in manipulating the world—that is, in plotting—allowed that aggression to make itself felt in a large, comprehensive action. The revenge plot enabled a single actor's flow of aggression to shape an entire, very complicated play.

∗   ∗   ∗

At its simplest level, the revenge plot was a way of linking corpses together. In 1588 this was exactly what the English theater needed. At the same moment that Kyd was discovering the revenge mechanism in *The Spanish Tragedy*, Marlowe was finding a relatively simple way to link corpses in *Tamburlaine*; the bodies there fall in a progression that makes a meaningful shape in our feelings, a profound gain over *Cambises*. But the revenge shape offers more complex possibilities, and like the Senecan rhetoric itself, helps deepen our response to the performer at the center. *Tamburlaine* is certainly a profounder and more lucid play than *The Spanish Tragedy*—one feels Kyd is nearly overwhelmed by the treasures he has stumbled upon—but the hero of *Tamburlaine* could never have the controlling relation to a complicated action that, for example, the main characters in *Henry IV, Part I*, enjoy, with their revenge-derived concern for action as intrigue: their strategy, manipulation, concealed aims, and weighing of possibilities. Nevertheless, Tamburlaine, though neither a revenger nor an intriguer, is also a Machiavellian hero, in the sense that he is an example of a man who rises solely through his own abilities. And the design of Marlowe's plot reflects this. *Tamburlaine* is a Machiavellian drama about political achievement in the secular world, and the sense of shape created by the series of triumphs for Tamburlaine and humiliations for his enemies comes from his carving out a design on the great world, a spectacular exercise of Machiavellian *virtù*. The plot allows us to feel the hero's presence thrusting out into—being articulated by—an all-shaping action, as if he could haunt every corner of the world. Thus the Senecan and Machiavellian influences join here, as in Kyd, to make the actor's powers felt. The plot goes resonantly with the great thrusting rhetoric that binds the world and its overarching stars to the psyche of the hero.

* * *

The powers of the actor determine the playwright's art, as the possibilities of language determine the poet's. To grasp this is to go a long way toward understanding drama, and it can save us from two opposed professional deformations that frequently distract us in dramatic theory—the actor's or director's prejudice against the written text, and the academic or literary prejudice against actors and directors. For the playwright's art, what he does with and through words, is an art of composing in the medium of the actor—of composing in action. A constant sensitivity to the "play" of the actor; a gift for placing him in a "world" that has the tensions and resonances of the audience's world but that while admitting them remains in some way protected from them; a closeness to the actor's relation to both worlds; an ability to keep the actor's most interesting processes constantly alive in the world of the play, to make the actor's freedom a source for action that engages, challenges, complicates, expands on our own awareness of freedom—by now it should be clear how essential these are—and always have been—to the playwright. We stand today at a moment when many workers in the theater seem to feel that the written script is dead, as if the playwright no longer had a place in the theater, or had somehow failed the actor. I don't think this is true, but it is clear that the ways of the actor change as the mind of the world changes. And just as a new way of placing the actor in an imagined world was needed in Marlowe's day, to make the most of the new relation of the actor to the mind of the world and to the figure of man in the mind of the world—just as Ibsen was able to imagine a modern actor in a modern action— so a similar leap of shaping imagination on the playwright's part seems needed—perhaps it would be better to say, possible—today. The leap needn't be the same for all playwrights or all actors, of course; and no one can fully imagine the leap before it happens, or even be sure of what is happening at the moment it occurs; but some types of exploration actors are making today seem to call out to playwrights for fulfillment. These experiments rise from developments in the actor's sense of his task, which parallel the changes already described in modern conceptions of the heroic role.

Acting is always changing, usually in relatively superficial matters of style—voice patterns, stances, degrees of literalness—but the important changes are those that affect our sense of what the actor shows us, especially of what he shows us that people who are not acting don't show. Discussion of this question tends to be confused, because whenever a new element is introduced into acting, when something new is shown by the actor, it is usually defended by being called "real"—but what is actually at stake is not greater or less fidelity to observable behavior, but the notion of what behavior is, what facts about human action drama is supposed to pursue.

Two radical changes of this kind have occurred in the past hundred years. In the latter part of the nineteenth century, the actor began to take on, to wear as a kind of living costume, a certain amount of specialized psychic equipment. Above all he had to become expert in what could be shown when something was not done. When Yeats complained of "modern educated people" that, "When they are deeply moved, they look silently into the fireplace," he was describing the necessary technique of a modern actor. The inner space that Ibsen and his successors were concerned with had to be charted by a repertory of pauses and indirections, by small details of gesture and expression—none of which perhaps was wholly original, but which now pointed to a new goal, a new sphere of action. The construction of plays, the technique of the actors, the age's growing interest in psychological science and in detection of all sorts, invited the audience to listen for movements beneath the characters' public performance, beneath even their consciousness. The actor devoted himself to what students of "the method" soon learned to call the "subtext." Subtexts of one kind or another had always existed, of course, but it is no accident that the idea of an emotional movement beneath the text, concealed by the text, was first carefully analyzed by Stanislavsky. For now the text itself was about subtextual life, and the new subtext was, even before Freud, a subtext of psychic secrets.

* * *

In the twentieth century, indeed very recently, acting has undergone, at least in some experimental groups, an even more radical change. An epistemological era has begun to produce an actor whose art is to explore the nature of acting itself. In the work of Peter Brook's latest phase, or that of Grotowski or the Open Theater, the actor presents himself as a man who has found his proper instrument of expression or, more typically, is in the process of finding it. His aim and subject are the true use of himself as such an instrument. This might seem to suggest that the actor is no longer "playing a part," that he has moved beyond the limits of drama as they are ordinarily understood. However, this kind of performance also requires a mask, a becoming-other, since the expression of self the actor seeks, even when he is not imitating any other person in his performance, is not of a kind to be observed, as such, in ordinary human relations or in the actor as he is in "real life," but only in the theater, before an audience, and through his artistic effort. He plays himself-as-actor.

The ontological leap characteristic of acting is always present in the work of such actors' groups. They wouldn't be actors if it weren't. More important, what they do wouldn't be acting. And though their art and theme would seem to constitute a break with traditional methods of assuming a character, their work—though it has so far proved of limited usefulness—vigorously exhibits that relation between the art of acting, the construction of drama, and the "outside" world that this chapter has tried to articulate. For what they offer us is a new way of finding in the powers and possibilities of acting a means for exploring our latest awareness of what is secret, fearful, and exciting in our experience. Consider, for example, *The Conference of the Birds*, with which Peter Brook's International Center for Theatre Research troupe recently visited America. The story of *The Conference of the Birds* is ostensibly drawn from a twelfth-century Sufi fable about the spiritual progress of a flock of birds as they journey toward the court of the emperor of birds, an enterprise which forces them to purge their souls of vanity and desire. But it is clearly the story of the actors' own discipline—how actors can find themselves, their proper freedom, their full expressiveness, by overcoming the tendency to show off, to play selfishly, superficially, vainly. In demonstration sessions before the performance, Brook invites his audience to join the actors in their exercises in communication, gesture, and movement. All of these, he explains, are designed to explore the resources of the actor, to help him discover and extend the limits of his expression, and also to put him in touch with what is genuinely his. The actors, for instance, are asked to walk and run about at various speeds and rhythms, trying, with every change, to maintain a full unstrained vitality in every part of the body. Or they sit on the floor and chant chorally in languages they do not know, trying to find the kinds of sound their bodies are capable of, separately and together, and what expressive force these sounds can carry. There are many related exercises in mime, acrobatics, and improvisation. Brook then shows us how, as part of these exercises, the actors work to express their imaginative awareness of "birds." They do not aim at superficial imitation, a rendering of the gait or cry of a particular creature, or even a full taking-on of his life. Garrick's superbly observant imitation of a turkey would be the very opposite of what they intend. They look into themselves, into the full repertory of the human, for the equivalents of what they understand as essential to bird movement, bird expression, bird life. And the process, as Brook tactfully makes us aware when he comments on our own efforts, is a spiritual discipline, involving simplification, concentration, purification—a labor that turns out to be very much like that of the birds in his story.

The play, on the night I saw it performed, was careless in detail and only intermittently interesting. But it helped make clear why this movement toward using the work of the actors' group itself as a subject for performance is natural for our time, can make a connection with what is most potent and unrealized in a modern audience's imagination, and thus carries with it the seeds of a powerful drama. For it places the actor in a world whose quality of freedom and exposure, danger and possibility, bears a disturbing resemblance to our own. The figure of the actor in his commune—or simply alone on the stage with us and his fellow actors—bending his narcissistic isolation and loneliness to the discipline of the excited, comforting, yet equally isolated group whose communion, though it may be deep, is always threatened by the potential falseness of acting itself, by the fragility of protection the group affords, and by the very temptation to further self-indulgence that lies within its comfort— this figure of the actor is expressive of one of our own most charged self-images. It might be described, in terms that link it to the images of man drama has always sought, as the image of a self free to act.

Acting—conceived as communal self-exploration, as "poor theater" in which freedom of expression is found in an abandonment of vanity, in a confrontation with the ironies of performance and role-playing—may strike us today as an avenue to individual truth and human achievement quite as real as any action in the great world is likely to be, and realer than most. We find it hard today to imagine heroic occupations, that is, occupations which can be filled with the haunting presence of a free man. When, as we often do, we describe human activity as "role playing," we usually mean not simply that we see our life as theater—many cultures have done so—but that we see it as boring theater, that we think of real life as a text so banal that no subtext—no individual movement toward freedom—can be expressed by it. All occupations strike us as specialties, as slots to be filled and skills to be accumulated. They belong to their technique; they cannot be ours. Any man of practical importance on the stage of the real world now seems an interchangeable part, like an astronaut. He is a statistic, a dependence, something predictable, depleted of humanity. And the changing sense of reality that has fostered this point of view is paralleled in the recent history of drama.

Behind the advent of "realism" in the nineteenth century—which meant not only literal portrayal but middle-class subject matter—lay an awareness that the traditional heroes of serious drama, remote and elevated figures, were becoming insignificant. Kings and generals were no longer important agents; if they were free at all, the only thing they were free from was inconvenience. History, economics, the will of constitutionally selected ministers, the laws of biology and physics determined their actions. Even the audiences of Scribe and Sardou knew that the fate of nations depended on glasses of water and scraps of paper. To imagine the life of a king or general, or even a glorious rebel, was not to escape into risk, autonomy, self-confrontation—it was merely escapism. In the twentieth century the process accelerated, and any character, even someone exactly like us, began to seem insignificant in the sense that audiences could no longer imagine him to be firmly embedded in the world, as Ibsen's characters—even Borkman and Rubek—are firmly embedded in the world of their plays. This difficulty led to the kind of hero I have described earlier, the hero who has fallen out of the world. And the falseness, pathos, exposure of his situation seemed to point more and more directly to the situation of the actor himself. The plays of Shaw, Brecht, and Pirandello, as we have seen, tend to create situations or styles in which the hero can be perceived, almost transparently, as an actor, almost as the actor who is playing him. Beckett and Pinter vary the effect by giving us actors who, while fully clothed in their roles, firmly embedded in a world (Pinter's more so than Beckett's, Didi and Gogo more so than Hamm and Clov), never let us know exactly what the role or where the world is. Thus we feel we're at a performance which resembles conventional drama—this is a world in some way copied from the literal appearances of the outside world, there is a *story* unfolding—but we're not out front somehow. We watch from the wings, we can't see all the scenery, we've missed something in the exposition, *maybe we don't belong to the world.* Perhaps the highly questionable term "absurd" may best be taken as referring to the common stylistic quality of plays that produce this effect: they heighten our sense of dispossession from the world by pretending that their characters imitate a coherent world, the principle of whose coherence is denied us.

Thus it is a natural step for drama to focus now not on the hero as actor, but the actor—this actor, here, tonight —as hero. The role of actor provides an image of freedom and risk, of human agency, that still has the power to strike us as genuine. The actor is free to be himself, to let himself loose in pursuit of his true expressive center. But this exalting freedom is dangerous, for many reasons—above all, because it involves play-acting, the abandonment of oneself unashamedly to all the possible falseness and corruption of performance, all the false roles, the mind-subduing systems we sense about us in the world. It is also dangerous because it invites not only falsification of the self, but destruction of the self in the rage for self-expression. This is the old Dionysian tension. And there is a further, a political, complication. The actor's thrust in all cultures is to claim a riveting significance for himself. It is impossible to act without saying *watch me.* One may attempt to offset this effect through unselfish ensemble playing, Brechtian detachment, discussions with the audience, etc., but the actor's special claim of significance remains, and it may present a terrible dilemma for the actor who is conscious of the claims of the oppressed, wary of complicity in exploitation. How is it possible, knowing what one knows today, to claim this kind of significance for oneself without diminishing the significance of those others who lie beyond the little society of actors and audience, without saying, in effect, *don't worry about them*? (Grotowski's actors seem to be struggling with this in their austere, ritualistic evocation of the death camps in *Akropolis.*) In another era, it might be easy to find many of these tensions in roles drawn from outside the theater, to locate this dangerous freedom in the "real world," but today our most sensitive impressions of life convince us that, all around us, reality is leaching· out of the world. As the *Marat/Sade* suggests, we cannot even imagine revolution in the profoundest possible way without at the same time acknowledging our dangerous and melancholy separation from reality. The soldier, the scientist, the lover, the political activist all seem compromised, not only insincere—drama has lived with that for some time—but denatured. Their power is not their own; they cannot *act*. The paradox of the actor, the exposed instability of his selfhood, now stands out as a guarantee of his humanity—and his labor to build a truth for himself and his peers upon the ruins of a compromised selfhood is likely to strike us as more genuine than the fates of kings or master builders. What the actor does is more like what a man who wishes to risk all might do. So the actor in his moment of communion with us may act in freedom, with all the risk and glory of the dramatic heroes of an earlier time. I think this is the possibility that has generated and sustained the best of such acting groups, and if none has come close to fulfilling it, if it remains only a possibility—and perhaps only one possibility among many—it is nevertheless an exciting one. Ultimate achievement will, I think, depend upon the genius of playwrights. The groups themselves, with their frequent indifference to the writer and their tendency to self-indulgence, are perhaps already a thing of the past. As I write this, the Open Theater has dissolved, and it is hard to imagine Brook's group continuing for long as presently constituted. But they have made their point. We look at performance differently because of them. Playwrights are responding to their example, actors have found a new skill, and the promise waits to be fulfilled.

* * *

An actor, whether he performs in the Theater of Dionysus at Athens or in Grotowski's Laboratory at Wroclaw, is always acting *something*. Some kind of script is always present—if not a written text, then a plan or idea for his performance, something that shapes and focuses his energy. Our sense, as an audience, of hero and play, of role and action, depends on what the actor and the script bring to each other. Looking back, we could say that this chapter has examined some of the ways in which a script mediates between the actor and the world. The flow of satisfactions in a dramatic performance both carries us deeper into the world and protects us from it. It allows us and the actors a special freedom, which has the power to evoke other deep awarenesses of freedom, of all that freedom threatens and is threatened by. The world we discover in the theater allows us at once an escape from self and a confrontation of self. But the connections we are seeking to understand, between the theater world and the rest of the world, finally will depend on what is distinctive about the theater world. We now are ready to consider more closely just how we perceive the world of the play, the activity of the actor, and the entire occasion of theater; how this perception differs from other types of experience; and, finally, why it is that our experience in the theater should seem to complete and extend our lives.

PART III

* * *

THEATER
AND
WORLD

--- * * * ---

"Theory" and "theater" derive from the same source. The theater is a *theatron*, a seeing place, but the kind of seeing involved is legitimately *theorein* as opposed to other seeing—an inspection, a looking at with a distinctive intensity, as a traveler or ambassador looks at things. Not a coming into the range of vision, nor a staring, but a process by which the mind inspects and possesses in inspection, as it possesses its own thoughts. The theater is thus, though not a place for contemplation, nevertheless a mind-place. For Plato and Aristotle, *theorein* was the mode for self-discovery or radical change.

* * *

What the mind inspects and possesses in the theater is action in performance in a scene, actors doing things in a special world which yet bears upon our own. The acting area is both a sacred field and a condensation of the known world, a place where the actor cannot die, the space where his gestures exhibit their eloquence because of the special charging of the place, because of its

113

investment with significance. The place exhibits the actors and holds the audience. It is always in some form a great reflector, helping to receive and throw back—as the performers receive and throw back—the aggressions of the audience.

Quasimodo has defined eloquence in poetry as "discourse with a world gathered up into a narrow landscape." Some intense condensation of the world is a feature of all literature. It is what William Empson has called "the pastoral," a landscape apparently small enough to be familiar and yet somehow containing the world. The actions of the Elizabethan hero gained resonance from being performed on a stage that had the recognizably condensed presence of the world. The same is true of the sacred bull's-eye of Greek drama and the balanced aquarium of fourth-wall realism. In this sense the physical setting of the theater—the theater building, stage, scenery—is a kind of eloquence itself, an eloquence at least *in posse* which the proper discourse can realize. It is a place for the mind, for "learning to think" in the sense that the symbolic play of a very young child is a way of learning to think—a place, that is, where we can assimilate freely so much that reminds us of the most traumatic adaptations.

∗   ∗   ∗

In the theater we enjoy a special relation not only to space but to time. Drama makes available, in the present, modes of experiencing that otherwise only refer to a past. What is present in a painting has already passed through somebody's eyes. The painter (at least) saw it—that painting, the very one you see. But nothing that goes on on a stage has been seen before you see it. There have been rehearsals, perhaps earlier performances—but not this one happening now. And yet what you see and the way you see are not like your ordinary experience of the present. They have a quality that the present does not give us elsewhere.

∗   ∗   ∗

Symbols refer either to a timeless state or to the past. For the medieval reader or the Platonist, the symbols of language could refer to what was eternal. Today, perhaps only the symbols of mathematics suggest an event or condition that is independent of a place in time. (Structuralism may be seen as a last-ditch attempt to recoup the eternity of mathematics for the word.) When we read literature today, we scan symbols that refer to events in the past or in something like the past. (It is something like the future too, since we imagine it on the basis of accruing memories rather than simply recall it—but it is not the present, not eternal, and not to be anticipated.) Put more simply, we go after the events in a novel, say, with the peculiar effort of trapping them in the mind that applies to occurrences that are not here-and-now but locatable in time. Drama, however, takes place in the present. We look directly at events which acquire, as we watch them, all the condensing power of symbols. They have a clarity we usually associate with retrospect, with mediation, but they are here-and-now, unmediated.

This is not quite true of dumbshow, or narrative mime, where the actor's body seems to become more transparent. Its presentness is diluted; we are being referred to an event, rather than confronted by its full bodily presence. This accounts for the use of dumbshow, especially in Elizabethan drama. There is a distinctive tonality to it, a narrative quality. Webster needs a pair of murders early in *The White Devil*, but he doesn't want us so fully involved with them as with the central presence of his heroine, so they are shown to us in dumbshow. We see them at a distance, the actors become symbols, representations of other people. Nowhere do we see better than in dumbshow how untypical of drama this kind of separation is, and how literary.

* * *

Literature is more like movies than drama, if we think of the author of a work of literature as a performer. His performance, like a movie actor's, takes place in an unreachable past. He is real, otherwise he could not have recorded these symbols, but by the nature of the medium he is not here-and-now. His verbal style is like the movie actor's star-quality, a perfected physiognomy which he brings to all encounters. What then of the author's words in a play? Or what indeed of language in drama? This is a delicate point, and only to be approached through the question of time. For it is the peculiar relation of language and time that accounts for the fact that while language is essential to the full life of drama, it is at the same time never quite at home on the stage. (Indeed language is never quite at home in the world, but that is another story.)

Movies again help suggest an answer. The problem of sound in films—the sense that, whatever has been gained, something has been lost in abandoning "silents"—rests in part on the fact that there is no aural equivalent to the convention that establishes our visual distance from the scene represented on the screen. We hear always from within the scene; we watch, in the movies, from outside it. What we see in life (and in the theater too, of course) tends to arrange itself on a flat plane; not so sound. Thus sound must violate the integrity of the flat movie picture. At the same time I can think of no silent picture (or talkie) which brings to the activity of talking itself the same absorbed and revealing gaze it lavishes on people doing other things like lighting cigarettes or dialing telephones. Talk, even when we cannot hear what is being said, diverts us from a concern with observing activity to a concern with interpreting symbols. In the theater the problem of sound is not the same. It is the power of sound to thrust forward and envelop the listener that makes the actor's voice so important a part of his bodily impression. The problem of talking, however, is similar. Language makes for drama, but speaking is in itself a non-dramatic act.

Speech is condensing, intensifying. It thrusts forward psychic states and at the same time brings them into a focused scene—but it breaks up presentness too. Speech makes activity into action, but while it shapes the action, the activity tends to stop. This is one of the reasons why excellent novelist's dialogue, which reads aloud well, and may even be an accurate transcript of real speech, tends to go dead on the stage. Speech is a problem in drama, and writing for the stage has always to struggle, to overcompensate, in order to maintain the necessary give and take of aggression, the flow of assumed and discarded disguises. Each line of dialogue must make up for what it destroys. (There are really three reasons why dramatic dialogue is under a special artistic burden. First, all speech tends to break us off from life in the present and set up another system of attention; it directs us to memory, interpretation, to other language. Second, all written dialogue, however colloquial, has been composed weeks, months, or years before we hear it spoken—but must not betray this, except for the purposes of deliberate irony. Third, much more must *happen* through conversation in drama than happens through conversation in ordinary life, where in fact conversation and real change very seldom go together—except on formal occasions, like trials and debates, both popular subjects for drama.)

There is a pastness to all language which is felt with special strength in the special presentness of the theater. In the theater, part of the struggle, actor's and writer's, is not to let the pastness appear. The problem is particularly intense in plays from earlier eras, where the remoteness of the idiom lays an extra burden of pastness on the present-day performer. We have a similar difficulty with literature, but novels and poems "date" far less drastically than plays, because in the theater there is always the danger of a split between language and the rest of the performance.

* * *

A few additional observations on the appetite for theater.

The transformation of eating into feasting and sex into love may be considered among the founding spiritual achievements of civilization. They are surely among the earliest and most important steps in creating a distinctly human culture. They make consciousness endurable and palatable, they convince the imagination that society has a "life." They are quasi-theatrical achievements, proceeding by role playing, spectacle, performance, plot.

Man is the theatrical animal in a primary sense. Animals imitate, animals pretend, but they do not play parts. Even politics is but an aspect of man's theatricality. The gift for performing as a character—and for playing the audience at such a performance—is no less extensive and characteristic of the human situation than the gift for language.

If the idea that society has a life—that it has a vital identity of its own that touches us and can enhance us—seems to require quasi-theatrical forms for its expression (feasting, courtship, family gatherings, elections, coronations, games), the life of society seems also to be one of the major concerns of drama. Not just in the obvious way, as subject matter, but as something felt both in the texture of performance and the theater occasion. All theater buildings dramatize the audience. They make society visible, a show in itself, condensed and displayed as the stage displays the actors. And some reorganization of the on-stage society (a new ruler, multiple marriages, general festivity, general woe) is a familiar concluding motif both in tragedy and comedy. Moreover, different plays and the drama of different eras establish different systems of relationship among the actors as an ensemble—the way they must share with, support, depend on, dominate, compete against each other, etc. while they perform—and our perception of this system is an important part of our experience of any play. I am glancing here at questions largely beyond the scope of this book, but another study of drama might profitably focus on the way several societies come together in the theater—the society of the culture at large, the society constituted by the audience, the society of actors on stage, and the society of the play-world in which the actors-as-characters move. (To which perhaps should be added the private or ghostly society, the inner cast of characters, that each member of the audience carries in his mind.)

* * *

All the unique qualities of awareness that theater makes available to us are finally best understood as contributing to a very special awareness of identity, a unique mode of experiencing both our own identity and that of others. We are responding to this when we use the word "identification" to describe what happens to us as we watch a play, but the word itself, as we commonly use it, obscures our response in the act of naming it. Once again our language, because of familiar, deceptive associations, works to cut us off from our theatrical experience rather than to clarify it. If "imitation" is a misleading term when it comes to thinking about drama, "identification" is at least equally treacherous—and perhaps even more important to get right. When we talk about an audience identifying with a character or about an actor identifying with the part he plays, we seem as a rule to make certain assumptions— certainly our language behaves as if we made them— about our own identities and our experience of the identity of acted characters in the theater. These assumptions are far from accurate, and they work to conceal a central truth about the nature of dramatic experience and the role it plays in our experience of the self. When we talk about identifying with a character in a play, we think of what we are doing as an instance of a process we imagine to be familiar from ordinary life—the charged, sympathetic way in which we experience our own identity and the moments when a similar sympathy enters into our awareness of others. "I identify with X," means, "I enter into X's life as into my own." The notion behind this is that our sense of our own identity not only reflects a unique focus of concern—this self is what we instinctively protect and extend, we thrill to its triumphs, etc.—but that this self is especially clear to us and that in moments of high imaginative activity or under the influence of a compelling dramatic performance, we enter into another's identity with a similar clarity.

But in fact this is not so. First of all, we experience actors-as-characters very differently from the way in which we experience people in ordinary life. We relate to the stage or playing area very differently from the way we relate to places and spaces in ordinary life, and we also relate differently to the people we see on the stage. Man is made present to the mind in the theater by an especially firm location of the performer in space and time; so firm that, in the theater, space and time take on a coherence that in "real life" we find it nearly impossible to perceive —space becomes a world and time becomes destiny. Moreover, man is present to us in drama with an ideal presentness. In spite of the excitements of performance, we see the people on stage with a relaxed clarity of attention that cannot be paralleled outside the theater, since certain distracting claims that other people inevitably make upon us in ordinary life do not apply. Outside the theater, the need to acknowledge and to be acknowledged by the people we encounter, the pressure of fear, responsibility, and uncertainty that we must feel in any person's presence, assures that time and space themselves are only blurrily felt and possessed by us.

To put it another way: One difference between actors in a theater and people we see on the street is that, whatever we may mean by the word, we identify more readily with the actors. We identify because we are free to do so, we are not threatened, as in life, by the otherness of other people. It is of course quite possible, in our daily affairs, to treat people as if they were merely performing for our entertainment; but the moral position and (unless we are lunatics) the experiential quality of such a relation is very different from our relation to actors on a stage. In the theater, the others we watch—frightening, exciting, touching as they are—can do no harm to us, and we can do nothing for them—we are not obligated to save Desdemona from Othello, because we can't. A man, performed by an actor, is so present that we can respond to his otherness, as we never quite can in real life, with a sense of freedom. In the theater, as perhaps otherwise only in our most intimate or illumined moments, the other's otherness is our joy and liberation.

Beyond this, the awareness we gain of the identity of actors-as-characters in the theater is *not* some less distinct echo of the way we experience our own. Rather it corresponds to a way in which we wish to perceive but necessarily fail to perceive our own identity, our own defining center of being, in ordinary life. For we are threatened by the pressures of otherness not only in our response to other selves but in our apprehension of our own. And here we come upon one of the reasons why the actor's art, that kind of mimesis so different from all other forms of mimetic activity, makes a special claim upon our imagination.

We are often told that from a psychoanalytic point of view the actor suffers typically from a failure to distinguish self from other, an "imperfect self-definition" or a "defective body-image" for which he tries to make up by acting. He identifies himself by impersonating another, establishes a self by escaping from the body of doubt that is the self. But this confusion about the self and about the body, the uncertainty that drives the actor toward his skill, is finally something all men bear, though the actor lives closer to it, keeps the wound open in order to heal it freshly in his art. Our personal sense of self is never the clear kind we imagine "others" have. For the self achieves its first identity in fear and deprivation. We do not know we have a self until we discover that it is not identical with the universe. To be aware of selfhood is to be aware of loss: You are merely a self, which is to say, something exposed—life with the rest of the world removed—assaulted by otherness from within and without. In taking on the spirit of another body, the actor leaps the gap between the fearful self and frightful other. He leaps it not in symbol or idea, as other artists do for their audiences, but in the very medium from which our self-confusion springs and in which it has its daily being—the medium of the charged, active, intimately present body. The actor is a figure of power and danger, of pity and fear, because he is at once the otherness that threatens—now uncannily animate—and the threatened self, daring in its exposure and ambition. We "identify" with the character he plays, with him-playing-the-character, because we respond to the energy with which he inhabits his new identity.

For a member of the audience, to become "identified" in the theater is at once to feel a magical sharpness of self-definition and to leap outside the area of threat, the arena of chaotic vulnerability in which our self-awareness always moves. "Identification" means, among other things, discovering identity. To share in the actor's achievement, to have a body-image free of "confusion" and "poor definition," is to be as a god or a spirit, endowed with the freedom of all that normally aggresses against the self, to take on the terrific selfhood of otherness.

* * *

This type of identification, then, is an essential characteristic of drama; it is inherent to the medium. Consequently, it will have a bearing on the effect and significance of any play. In fact, I would suggest that the covert theme of all drama is identification, the establishment of a self that in some way transcends the confusions of self. The action of any play, all that its characters "go through," is a way of discharging and expressing the hidden burden of threat that these confusions always carry.

* * *

It is easy to see that, in a superficial sense, the discovery of identity is very often an explicit subject of drama, never very far from the surface of most plays we care about. We may think of Oedipus finding out who he is; or Everyman learning what his real possessions are; or Lear recognizing that he is a foolish fond old man; or Jack and Algy discovering how important it is to be named Ernest. But identification, in the sense I have defined, is far more broadly and deeply influential than this.

Even plays which obviously have to do with questions

of identity in the superficial sense seem to yield up more of their mystery to our understanding if we think of them in the light of the process of identification. The famous irony of *Oedipus Rex*, for example, springs directly from Oedipus's characteristic self-assertion, a connection frequently overlooked or misunderstood. The force of the irony is not we-know-something-you-don't-know or ooh-what's-going-to-happen-to-him, but a re-vision of familiar activities in an unfamiliar light. We respond to Oedipus's strong, aggressive, self-defining drive—his hearty energy of inquiry, civic pugnaciousness, love of difficult puzzles, thrust to mastery—but they all acquire a new tonality because we know the horrible end to which they are unknowingly directed. The thrust to self-definition changes tonally for us because of the situation, and we are able to see the action in two ways at once: Oedipus defining himself in the present, as he and his subjects understand him, and Oedipus defining himself in the future as his fate demands and only *we* begin to know. One could say that the irony allows the future itself to function like a character. Oedipus defines himself by carrying on a dialogue with the future, and the richness of the irony comes not from his simply invoking doom on his head and not knowing it, but by the interaction between the various styles in which he invokes it (rational, pious, political, murderous) and the future we know.

But although we know the future we do not know *his* future—the final interaction. We know what Oedipus will find out, but we do not know how he will define himself against the discovery. Thus the early richness of irony leads to an unexpected later richness. The early irony rises from the interaction between the tremendous self-defining impulse that characterizes Oedipus—his manic, confident desire to know, to see, to solve—and what we know he will see if he persists in searching. The later richness comes when we discover that this same amazing individual energy, an energy that specifically insists on the individual (I, Oedipus, alone do things this way), will continue unabated, even intensified, right up to and beyond his discovery of the truth. Now, this is the kind of truth that is supposed to crush the individual life out of the discoverer, since it shows him absolutely subject to fate; but in the case of Oedipus, of course, it does not. Thus the dialogue with the future by which Oedipus defines himself, producing a richness of irony because he does not know *how* he defines himself, becomes a richness of self-assertion, a dialogue on equal terms with fate, once he knows all.

Sophocles makes clear—what presumably was not at all clear in the myth—that although Oedipus was fated to murder his father and sleep with his mother, he was not fated to know that he had done so, that in fact he insisted on knowing it in spite of increasingly desperate counsels to back off, to avoid the discovery. Oedipus discovers the truth because truth tempts him, because he insists on exercising his powers. Even after he finds out the truth, he goes on asking questions; and at the very end he is still giving orders—for his banishment.

∗   ∗   ∗

The identification Oedipus achieves at the end of his play—the sense we get of a self established beyond and in the teeth of the deepest confusions of self—points to another way in which identification governs the processes of tragedy. One requirement of successful tragedy seems to be that the defining energies of the hero—the actor-like freedom he pursues—must be matched to the catastrophe in a manner that is both convincing and surprising. In some sense, we must feel he has sought out the right death or disaster, the one that completes his definition. Greek tragedy perhaps states the problem most baldly.

Consider simply the spectacle as the tragic process starts. In the center of the ring, an outsize image of a man moves toward the altar, where, earlier, we have seen the performance begin with a sacrifice to Dionysus. We are far from the hero. A good portion of the entire city's population sits around us. We all look down the vast cupped slope into the stone bull's-eye, the dancing ring with an altar at the center. The man walks on high shoes, his voice booms loudly with a metallic ring through the outsize suffering mask. He is a hero, a king and warrior familiar to us from the fables of our childhood and the ordinary language of the town. We know all about him as he moves toward the bull's-eye reciting grandly. We are waiting for him to be destroyed. Like any audience we are aware that a kind of contract exists between the playwright and ourselves; the opening movements of the play (and, in Greece, the very occasion of the festival) have aroused expectations the playwright must undertake to satisfy. Here, however, the size and sculptural clarity of the forms, the intense civic and religious focus, the definiteness of the convention heighten the contract's risk and promise, which in turn parallel that of the actor and the hero. Here, as finally in any tragedy, the risk and promise, focused in the exposed extremism of the actor's self-assertion, cry out for the character's destruction—but it must be (and the theory of tragedy exists largely to explain the phrase that follows) exactly the right destruction.

The sense of appropriate climax by which we instinctively judge tragedy (whether we call it "calm of mind all passion spent" or "the catharsis of pity and fear") must come from a proper adjustment of destruction and identification. That is, although the actor is finished off in some way—usually killed—our awareness of him at the moment of death and after must resemble in strength and completeness our earlier awareness of him-in-the-part with his definite, steadily projected identity. His catastrophe and the final action of the play must fix him for us in the gesture of a complete unfolding. His death, if death is the result, will have identified him—not in the sense that he is the man who died this way, but in the sense that these shocks were necessary to exhibit his full genius. In the same way, Oedipus is not the man who murdered his father, married his mother and found out about it, but the man who sought out and met this fate in a fully self-unfolding way.

The Elizabethan theater lacked a curtain, so Shakespeare was compelled to get his dead heroes off the stage some way or other, but the processions with which his tragedies end are much more than conveniences; they are spectacular gestures of identification. With the accompanying speeches, they work to display the dead hero to the audience, as if to show how achieved and satisfying the final chord has been, in spite and because of the destruction we have witnessed—to give full resonance to the massed, intricate harmony of feelings toward character, actor, and play that has been built around the hero at his death. When the play is over, we make our way toward an exit, the gestures and rhythms of the hero governing our bodies as we walk, but included now in the larger, simpler tread of the dead march and the final words of sorrow and exaltation, the two rhythms preserving, extending, perfecting each other. Watching them bear Hamlet off, we have thought about Hamlet. All the shocks he has been heir to, all the entanglements of thought and feeling his meditations and the plot have put him through, have combined to leave him definite, strange, and controlling, like an actor on the stage of our memory. The destructive action of the play has saved a self from chaos, established it beyond the chaos to which we now return.

* * *

Comedy seems to be fascinated by questions of identity, and this surface interest reflects a deeper concern with identification. Conventionally and indefatigably, comic action pursues revelations of identity, the throwing off of disguises, the establishment of long-lost selves and relations—the ultimate marriages, reunions, and successes that form the traditional denouements of comedy. But this familiar pattern, which runs through dramatic history from Plautus to the latest Broadway musical, simply captures and directs the strong impulse toward identification that the traditional hero of comedy always has, an impulse, usually, toward sexual winning-through. The young man of classical comedy, pursuing the girl through a tangle of deceptions and family restraints, pitted against the obduracy or mean-spiritedness of the older generation, is basically out to establish himself as an adult—and, until he does, the trick of the plot is to balance every move he makes toward sexual fulfillment with some catastrophe that places him in the role of naughty boy threatened with punishment. The Plautine plot may be described as a device for transforming the shifts of a naughty boy into the triumph of an adult male.

Comedy draws much of its pleasure from direct celebration of the assimilative powers of dramatic performance, flaunting the protectedness of the play-world, the getting-away-from-threat that acting and theater, disguising and playing a part allow. Thus comedy has always thrived on extravagant elaborations of theatrical process, on the overflow of theatrical devices into relatively realistic situations ("Quick, get into this laundry basket!"), and on the eruption of the actor's process of identification in its most obvious and insistent forms ("Herman, say you're my aunt!") into the plot of the play. Mistaken and ultimately revealed identity, the dance and game of masks, are staples of comic design.

At the same time, great comedy has always seemed inclined to talk (if only parenthetically) about the deeper meaning of what it is playing with, to touch on—and make further play out of—the problems of finding and maintaining identity, of establishing the self in the real world. *The Importance of Being Earnest*, which parodies any number of dramatic conventions, carries the insouciance of comedy to a satirical extreme by making the discovery of the heroes' first names the point of the entire action. If the plot is a joke about Victorian earnestness, it is also a joke about drama's earnest pursuit of revealed identity.

Self-discovery is of course a regular theme of Shakespearean comedy, especially the major comedies. All of them are shaped by a strenuous and specific exploration of sexual identity, which makes great play not only out of the establishment of self but of the tensions and confusions to which the effort toward self-definition is exposed. Shakespeare's comic heroes generally begin in a state of withdrawal from the world—as the heroes of *Love's Labor's Lost* start off by establishing an academic utopia from which women are banished, or as the Duke in *Twelfth Night* begins by refusing all normal activity for a hopeless and self-indulgent melancholy. But sexual withdrawal in Shakespeare is invariably challenged and criticized by dramatic encounter. The closed-off adolescent who in the sonnets and *Venus and Adonis* is both threatened and tested by the presence of a lustful female, is forced in most of the comedies (as in *Romeo and Juliet*) to open himself to a greater realism and vitality, represented by a lively intelligent woman, rather more sensible

than he is, passionate in her affections but free of
narcissistic and romantic illusion. Very often she exhibits
her superior realism, her ability to deal with passion and
obstacle, by taking on male costume, which (rather like
the transvestism of many initiation ceremonies) reflects
not sexual confusion on her part but a firm sense of
sexual identity. The self-possessed and risk-taking hero-
ines of the early plays lead their men out into a world of
danger and commitment, which Shakespeare associates
with wisdom, pleasure, sexual fulfillment, and significant
action. Throughout these plays there runs an undercurrent of discussion on the theme of identification, specifically on the movement of the self into its proper sphere
of definition; this is the sphere of commitment and
encounter, where one must—as Bassanio correctly
guesses in *The Merchant of Venice*—"Give and hazard all
he hath" to win through to the happy ending.

Shakespeare seems aware that even the most farcical
manipulations of comedy have to do with the search for
identity and with the chaos of confused self-images that
seems always to threaten the self. His earliest comedy,
The Comedy of Errors, is a farce about mistaken identity,
and there Shakespeare improves on the plot that he
borrows from Plautus by multiplying the already abun-
dant confusions available in his source. (He gives the
long-separated twin heroes twin servants, also long separated, to attend them.) Moreover, Shakespeare adds to
the bewilderments his heroes suffer a note of magic and
madness which heightens the feeling of identity thrown
comically into chaos; and—very lightly but definitely—he
adds a deeper note of meditation on the loss of self, the
search for self:

ANTIPHOLUS: Farewell till then. I will go lose myself,
              And wander up and down to view the city.

MERCHANT: Sir, I commend you to your own content. *Exit.*
ANTIPHOLUS: He that commends me to mine own content
Commends me to the thing I cannot get.
I to the world am like a drop of water
That in the ocean seeks another drop,
Who, falling there to find his fellow forth,
Unseen, inquisitive, confounds himself.
So I, to find a mother and a brother,
In quest of them, unhappy, lose myself.

This deeper note, suggesting that, for Shakespeare, comedy always shadows forth a grave search for self, is heard with increasing resonance throughout his work. Nowhere is it more evident than in his last play, *The Tempest*, where old Gonzalo sums up the action as follows:

> O, rejoice
> Beyond a common joy, and set it down
> With gold on lasting pillars: in one voyage
> Did Claribel her husband find at Tunis,
> And Ferdinand, her brother, found a wife
> Where he himself was lost, Prospero his dukedom
> In a poor isle, and all of us ourselves
> When no man was his own.

The *Taming of the Shrew*, to take a final and in this context unfamiliar example, a masterpiece so easy and robust that we seldom give it a second thought, reveals a remarkable concern, both in its formal design and its treatment of character, with the psychology of sexual identity. Shakespeare juxtaposes the relatively academic comedy of Bianca and her suitors with the more popular high jinks of Petruchio's wooing of Kate, and the effect is to sharpen and deepen the theme of sexual winning-through. Compared with Petruchio, the other wooers hold back from the full stress of sexual involvement. Lucentio prefers the conventionally submissive Bianca to the up-

setting Kate, while Hortensio, upon discovering that ·
Bianca favors Lucentio, flies into a pet and marries an
accommodating widow. At the play's end, it is of course
clear that only Petruchio has really "tamed" a wife.
Bianca's young suitors, one notices, have living fathers to
contend with, and they all settle for wives who to some
extent master them. Petruchio's father is dead; he is his
own man, and—like the style of his part of the play—he is
rougher and realer than the rest, more direct in his
sexuality. Throughout the comedy, Shakespeare plays on
the contrast between stage illusion and life illusion,
realistic and conventional styles, effective and ineffective
play-acting. Petruchio tames Katharina because, through
his role-playing and plotting, he is able to force her both
to acknowledge his identity and to discover her own. The
joke-form of this shows Petruchio, apparently, as a crude
male supremacist; he compels Kate to agree that, if he
says so, the sun must be the moon. But the deeper
emotion we get from the taming scenes suggests that
Petruchio is able to appeal to Kate as a man and accept
and confront her as a woman, while she, through his
intervention, is able to break out of her narrow "shrew-
ish" role, and get away forever from her father's house
and the passive tyranny of her goody-goody younger
sister.

*   *   *

The action of even the lightest comedy must always be a
tearing apart. Soothing conventional boulevard entertainment (Maugham's *The Constant Wife*, say, or the latest
Broadway descendant) offers us very nicely set up identities, fluent successes in a comfortable world—but how
dull they would be, how impossible it would be to *make*
the identification, if the action didn't put the identification
in jeopardy. That is why, even on Broadway, the plot
must come up to certain standards which are technically

very exacting. However airily, the plot must expose the characters to situations or frustrations that are intolerable, in the sense that they threaten the characters' self-definition with collapse. They would be publicly humiliated, cut off from their one true love, disowned, stripped of the Crunchies account, whatever. Not necessarily the gravest consequences, but intolerable to them —sufficient in terms of the play-world utterly to tear apart the fabric from which their comfortable, fully asserted self is made. In most light comedy, anything like the tearing apart we encounter in real life would destroy the play, introduce questions that cannot be entertained, strip away the protection; but nevertheless we must have a crisis in which we can feel the tearing-apart energy leaping around the theater in the form, say, of a nifty reversal, or a spasm of activity, or a finely sustained embarrassing pause—ready to be echoed, finally, in the violence of our laughter. So in its own terms, even commercial fluff must have its *sparagmos*.

It's as if the terrificness of the actor could reach us only through the pressure of the action on him, as if the basic human confusion which taints all awareness of self, and which draws us to the theater and its identifications in the first place, had to be re-enacted in order to make the identification occur. At any rate, without an action that somehow makes the actor-as-character risk destruction of his constructed self, his leap of self-definition cannot be extended to the audience. Admittedly it's amazing what low levels of dramatic energy commercial audiences can put up with, but I suppose this only suggests how strong the appetite for identification is and how intense and deeply buried are the fears that lie behind it. To take on the matinee idol's uncomplicated freedom, while letting risk in in only the most protected and flattering form, is for many people simply the best bargain available.

* * *

A word about identification and the *Verfremdungseffekt*. Brecht's major characters are survivors, and they play the system's games in order to survive in it. Garga outdoes Shlink at ruthlessness, Shen Te disguises herself as the landlord, Shui Ta, Mother Courage carries on business as usual amid the big business of war. The self-definition they achieve through the action of their plays constitutes a criticism of the system as well as an imitation of it. Brecht's concluding image of Mother Courage pulling her cart is a fully unfolded expression of her energy and misery and of the back-breaking bleakness of the order she serves. She is almost completely unaware of the criticism, but like Shen Te and Garga, her development through the play, the self-assertion she makes through the action, clearly expresses the system's inhumanity, and clearly projects her own character as created by the system and baffled by it, defined because seen against the background of the system.

The acting technique Brecht advocates enables the actor to achieve two effects, which must be understood as simultaneously present in his performance. First, he must express the character he portrays with, inevitably, some degree of realism, but he must also manage to stay outside the system of realistic portrayal and comment upon it. It is the second effect we usually have in mind when we describe a performance as Brechtian, and it does represent Brecht's major contribution to acting theory; but his writings on the theater make clear that *both* are necessary to the work of the actor, and surely both are implicit in the text of his plays. Just as the Brechtian character is in, but not of, the system, so the Brechtian actor is fully involved and yet at a critical distance from his part. The alienation effect is appropriate to characters who are socially alienated. It is a way of achieving identity that reflects and heightens the paradox of a character whose identity, fully revealed, shows him to be a victim of the system he "identifies with."

∗ ∗ ∗

Identification, then, is a triple mechanism. It is the process by which *we* take pleasure in the uniquely defined character moving before us. It is the process by which *the actor* takes on another life. And finally it is the process by which *the character* in the play defines himself through and against the action.

The three processes will always be connected. Many of Stanislavsky's recommendations for building a character, for example, are particularly suited to a certain kind of naturalistic play, in which the major characters are compelled to discover or reveal a complex of subtextual secrets that define their situation, and in which the main action turns on this discovery. Thus, in *Rosmersholm*, Rosmer and Rebecca West discover for us layer after layer of motivation, memory, and hidden feeling—exactly the elements that any actor of these roles would have to call upon, to work back to, to prepare the part. Ibsen's characters generally pursue a connection with the past, whose significance they have kept secret from themselves or others—some buried impulse, perhaps, or obscure goal, or even a scrap of what Stanislavsky would call "emotional memory." Hilda Wangel, for instance, represents all three of these for Solness in *The Master Builder*. And, as the example of *The Master Builder* suggests, if the characters are not busily pursuing the hidden burden of the past, the action makes it pursue them, challenging their self-definition, as Hilda pursues and challenges Solness.

In many plays of the last hundred years, the actors, the characters, and the audience are jointly engaged in uncovering at least one character's motivation. Just as

Lee Cobb had to construct Willy Loman out of details that built up a portrait of Willy's family history, buried recollections, and controlling desires, so Miller's play works by the same method to define his hero for the audience. Both the actor and the action must tunnel backwards and forwards toward that night in Boston, gathering as they go the fragments of a defining portrait of Willy's psyche.

Building a character in Stanislavsky's terms—arriving at an inner truth of will or compulsion by studying all the forces that govern a character's behavior—parallels the major processes by which characters are identified in modern realistic drama. To follow out the exploration of a character's motivation and his past in psychological, physical, and social terms, to pursue the means by which a "method" actor may identify with Hedda Gabler or Willy Loman, is not only to "prepare" the part; it is to trace the effect of the play's action as it identifies the character in the audience's mind. Not every great performer of these roles will be a method actor, of course, but one way or another his identification will inevitably encompass these determining materials, because the play insists upon them.

* * *

Sometimes the relation between the three mechanisms of identification—actor's, audience's, and character's—is so clear, as in *Death of a Salesman*, say, that to consider them separately at any length would be redundant. In other cases, however, the connection is not so obvious, and here careful attention to one mechanism can help reveal the nature of the rest. The *Marat/Sade*, for instance, is "Brechtian" in that, most of its action being a play within a play, its actors necessarily stand at a distance from their roles. This effect is heightened by the use of verse narrative and song, by the frequent interruption and discussion of the performance, by the attention constantly drawn to the disparity between the inmates and the parts they play. Yet Peter Brook, in preparing for his great production, required his actors to spend weeks studying the behavior of the insane, and the result was an accuracy of inner and outer detail in the finest naturalistic vein. We "believed in them" as madmen. Brook did not scant the Brechtian texture, however, and while most actors had, in the nature of their roles, to stress one or the other approach in their performance, most needed to call on both processes to a noticeable degree.

Brook was right; Weiss's text demands both a Brechtian and a naturalistic technique. The actor who plays Marat must be a paranoiac, dozing and rousing in his tub, but he must also be the stylized, selective version of a revolutionary leader Weiss-de Sade has created. The two portrayals must be connected, of course, but they are in no simple sense one. The actor who gives the speeches simply in the character of the paranoiac will fail as surely as the one who neglects to be a convincing inmate. The revolutionary voice both is and is not the madman's. The actor must achieve identification by two means, which comment upon each other.

Charlotte Corday's lover, Duperret, is likewise both a comic caricature of bourgeois reaction and a believable erotomaniac. As a distancing device, the erotomania provides a brilliant satiric comment on counter-revolutionary "idealism" and "humanism," but it must also be realistically portrayed. Duperret must perform convincingly as yet another member of the lunatic chorus, and it is their precisely rendered desperation and desire that gives conviction to their performance as the revolutionary mob.

The actors' methods of identification will, of course, deeply affect our perception of the action and of the idea of revolution. We plainly are meant to sympathize with the revolutionary spirit in the play. We want it to succeed; we laugh bitterly at its betrayal. And we are on the madmen's side too (especially because they give such excellent performances in de Sade's play). Coulmier, the asylum's director, is our enemy. But the desires and deformities of the madmen, portrayed as they are with such precision, intensity, and appeal, are terrifying as well as fascinating.

Our response to the madmen is affected by a third process of identification, which may be associated with the name of Artaud. All the elements of what Artaud calls "the theater of cruelty" are present. The convulsive choric movement, the savage abandon of the mob, the blood, violence, and extremity of gesture—all require an additional calculation on the part of actor and director. Like the other processes, it affects the audience's identification with the characters. The naturalistic process offers us an identity located inside the system of feelings of the individual madmen. The Brechtian process identifies us with the position of someone outside the system the madmen portray as actors in de Sade's drama, someone who observes its workings and contradictions. The Artaudian system identifies us with an overwhelming choric drive breaking down individual personality. I am aware that in some sense any play may be separated into these three components—this might, in fact, form the basis of a useful method of dramatic analysis. But clearly in the *Marat/Sade* the systems exist in an articulated separateness, and the play's effect on us comes from the juxtaposition and mutual support of the different kinds of identification they provide.*

---

* In his introduction to the English translation of the play, Brook himself seems to recognize only two systems, the Brechtian and the Artaudian, which he also calls "subjective." "Subjective" is perhaps a

To put it simply will require summing up complex responses in terms of political idea, and I am sure—the politics at issue being so incendiary, the freedoms glanced at so central and disturbing to our current understanding of the world—that the terms I attach will seem questionable to many. I shall be satisfied if they are taken simply as approximations, an attempt to articulate the chord of response the multiple systems create. So: The revolution is presented *as a performance* in the *Marat/Sade*, but the mental state of the performers is naturalistically observed and re-created by the actors. While the revolution-as-performance is thus "unreal" and we are distanced from it, beneath the performance we are aware of an impulse that, especially by contrast, we feel to be that of reality itself. Beneath history (debatable, artificial, ironically perceived) is madness—ourselves. We see the people of Paris as actors in a script, parts of a savage diagram of social forces; but we also understand their inner life as individual madmen—their motivations, their inner movements, are transmitted to us; beyond this, we respond chorically to their force as an outraged mob.

The situation of an audience assimilating these different appeals to self-projection, to clarification of self, may be likened to de Sade's image of the young novices at Charlotte Corday's convent, asleep in the summer night:

> Imagine
> those pure girls lying on hard floors

---

way of letting in what I call the naturalistic system. But I think it is important to point out that a recognizable element of naturalistic preparation is required if the play's "Artaudian" impact is to be achieved, as Brook's own production demonstrated. The play demands performances that (1) build up large convulsive effects resembling those Artaud describes in *The Theater and Its Double*, and (2) offer us convincing, if selectively realistic, portraits of individual inmates of Charenton. Part of the genius of Weiss's creation is that so much of (1) is able to develop naturally from (2). The play's concreteness of reference gives it a force many exercises in both "alienation" and "cruelty" lack.

in rough shifts
and the heated air from the fields
forcing its way to them through the barred windows
Imagine
them lying there
with moist thighs and breasts
dreaming of those
who control life in the outside world.

All the play's modes of identification are evoked here: a close-to feeling of individual desire and sensation; a gathering pressure of instinctual energy; and interwoven with these, a more mediated vision of politics, of "the outside world." We respond to the inmates' subjective life both as pathetic individual feeling and overwhelming choric impulse, and yet, at the same time, watching their performance of de Sade's play, distanced from the Revolution by their technique, we "dream" of the larger powers that shape the course of history.

A main connecting term between what the inmates do and what they represent is the tub in which the actor who plays Marat constantly bathes. Marat and the inmate who plays him both need hydrotherapy; each is a prisoner of a disease. Marat's radical "call to the people" and his ineradicable itch twine together in our minds. As with de Sade, the philosophy and the bodily longing, the madness and the performance, both reinforce and undermine each other.

Another example of the play's powerful mixture of styles may be found in the way Weiss plays off Duperret against Jacques Roux, when Roux—wearing a straitjacket, as he does throughout the play—is first introduced:

> (DUPERRET *approaches* CORDAY, *pawing her furtively.
> The* HERALD *raps him on the hand with his staff. A*
> SISTER *pulls back* DUPERRET.)

HERALD: Jailed for taking a radical view
      of anything you can name the former priest
      Jacques Roux
(*indicates* ROUX *who pushes out his elbows and raises his head*)
      Ally of Marat's revolution but
      unfortunately the censor's cut
      most of his rabble-rousing theme
      Our moral guardians found it too extreme
ROUX: Liberty
(*opens his mouth and pushes his elbows out vigorously.* COULMIER *raises his forefinger threateningly.*)

The analogy is two-edged. Roux's doctrine is subverted by the suggestion that it is a mania like Duperret's, but we are also readier to see Duperret (and by extension all bodily desires) as a victim of oppression. Roux, like Marat's tub, is a connecting term, since his "madness" seems to consist in radicalism. It is perhaps a lunatic radicalism—we are never quite sure—but it is clear that he has been locked up because he insists on talking about revolution. Here again the systems of identification required of the actors work together to insure a richness of emotional and intellectual response. If one process of the play succeeds in condensing all revolution to a madman's cry, the other process makes us experience the cry as our own.

∗ ∗ ∗

Shakespeare's Cleopatra offers a different example of how the concept of identification helps cast light on a challenging dramatic text. Cleopatra is clearly a superb acting role—but she has never ceased to cause difficulties for performers and scholars alike. There is a tradition of discussing the part in terms of the capacities of the Elizabethan boy-actor, which today might seem to be an utterly academic issue. Surprisingly though, it offers a way to the heart of the role's difficulty, and this is because it raises the question of identification. Few scholars would now agree with the once-fashionable notion that Cleopatra simply could not have been adequately played by a boy; but current opinion seems to be divided between Granville-Barker's position that the role is carefully tailored to the boy-player's technical limitations and the position ably argued by Michael Jamieson that we cannot be at all sure as to what, if any, those limitations were, since the part is intensely demanding of mature emotional and sexual expression. Actually, each of these interpretations responds to something Shakespeare wrote into the play. Their apparent disagreement can be resolved and the analysis carried a step further if we approach the role with identification in mind.

When we study the role of Cleopatra as an actor might, we discover that the dominant style of her dialogue—and the emotional qualities which the style reflects—do not remain the same throughout the play. In fact as the action progresses the role increasingly presents a challenge to what the play itself urges us to think of as the boy-actor's skills. My point is that Cleopatra's development as a character is reinforced by a process which makes us feel that the boy-actor is moving beyond the limits of his art. The effect will also appear in an actress's performance, where it will come across as movement from one style of self-presentation to a more demanding one. This process of identification accompanies and supports the process by which Cleopatra, the character, transcends the threats to her conception of greatness that defeat and death have posed.

It is not at all a question of whether the part is in any way actually beyond the limits of most boy-actors, but that it is *felt* to stretch and go beyond them. The audience will have to believe that this has been accomplished if, in the final act, it is to accept Cleopatra's contemptuous and audaciously explicit

> The quick comedians
> Extemporally will stage us, and
> . . . I shall see
> Some squeaking Cleopatra boy my greatness
> I' th' posture of a whore.

Cleopatra, as Antony says, is a woman whom everything becomes, and she makes more and more become her as the play moves on; but at first what becomes her is to chide, to weep, to wrangle, to shift emotions quickly, to flirt, to make quick, teasing, pointed remarks. Some early flashes may arguably require or sustain a deeper emotional undercurrent, but what is certain is that, as the play develops, such breakthroughs become more marked. Her rage at the messenger who brings news of Antony's marriage in the second act may be one of these—a dangerous power can come through here—but she quickly enough returns to the typical boy-wit. A clearer case of change occurs late in the third act, when she rejects Antony's accusation of disloyalty:

> Ah, dear, if I be so,
> From my cold heart let heaven engender hail,
> And poison it in the source, and the first stone
> Drop in my neck: as it determines, so
> Dissolve my life; the next Caesarion smite
> Till by degrees the memory of my womb,
> Together with my brave Egyptians all,
> By the discandying of this pelleted storm, .
> Lie graveless, till the flies and gnats of Nile
> Have buried them for prey!

Not only the subject matter but the way the images are linked and developed demands a more entire and extended giving of a passionate self, in no way helped by playfulness or epigrammatic phrasing. It has her old extravagance, but its proliferating richness of metaphor reminds us of Antony's "Let Rome in Tiber melt, and the wide arch/ Of the rang'd empire fall!"

It is a great mistake, though a common one, for an actress to fail to strike the "boyish" note—pert, piquant, witty, words well forward in the mouth—that Shakespeare gives to Cleopatra at the start, and never entirely abandons. The qualities that distinguish Cleopatra in the first act never disappear, but are subsumed, as the play proceeds, into a more complex verbal and emotional organization.

Cleopatra dominates the play after Antony's death at the end of the fourth act, and her language in the great final scenes retains all the striking verbal habits that dazzle us in the early acts—speed of association, suddenness of wit, deftness of aggression. Now, however, they are not governed by epigram, flirtatiousness, or chiding. The pattern of language is more complex and extensive, the feeling more expansive and demanding:

> Give me my robe, put on my crown, I have
> Immortal longings in me. Now no more
> The juice of Egypt's grape shall moist this lip.
> Yare, yare, good Iras; quick: methinks I hear
> Antony call. I see him rouse himself
> To praise my noble act. I hear him mock
> The luck of Caesar, which the gods give men
> To excuse their after wrath. Husband, I come:
> Now to that name, my courage prove my title!
> I am fire and air; my other elements
> I give to baser life. So, have you done?
> . . . Have I the aspic in my lips? Dost fall?
> If thou and nature can so gently part,
> The stroke of death is as a lover's pinch,
> Which hurts, and is desir'd.

The passage is full of swift accesses of her old wit ("Have I the aspic in my lips?"), and the great actress will make the most of them; but they are now most poignant in effect and serve only to sharpen our impression of how far Cleopatra has traveled in her journey toward death.

Earlier in the scene, Cleopatra has prepared us for this passage, and for the scene of suicide to follow. But she has done so by alerting us to comparisons which will either make her performance seem weak by contrast or set it off in impressive relief, depending on whether the actress or boy-actor can live up to the opportunities Shakespeare has supplied. First, she has scornfully referred to the inadequacies of the squeaking boy-actors who will attempt to portray her in Rome. And she has gone on to invite another potentially damaging standard by which to measure the performer's achievement:

> go fetch
> My best attires. I am again for Cydnus
> To meet Mark Antony.

This reminds us of Enobarbus's earlier lengthy, extravagant word-picture of a superhumanly attractive Cleopatra in her barge on Cydnus ("The barge she sat in like a burnish'd throne . . ."), which now the performer must match in person. Once more it is a situation in which the actress or boy-actor is required to remind us of his apparent limitations, and overcome them. At the end of the play, Cleopatra insists on herself as woman, empress, mother, and wife, and as something like a deity, as someone very like Antony in his final transfiguration, rather than the girl-like consort of the early acts. The actor's achievement in tracing this development—his identification with the role—becomes in Shakespeare's hands a felt metaphor for the liberating greatness and inclusiveness, the triumph over limit, that Cleopatra achieves in her last hours.

* * *

Shakespeare is unparalleled in his capacity for subtly highlighting and exploiting the actor's process of identification so as to suggest the richness of self-definition that his characters achieve in crucial scenes. This becomes especially notable precisely at moments when the actor might be tempted to let his performance become "bitty," to play for the surface value of a highly separable speech or passage. For instance, toward the end of many Shakespearean tragedies, the hero appears to "revert" to an earlier stability or noble self-definition. This is frequently interpreted as a reassertion of mislaid dignity or virtue, which may be accurate enough, but these moments also carry a more complex burden of meaning and feeling. We can do them further justice if we recognize that, when they occur, the poise the actor achieves must always express and control a number of serious threats to that poise, which have emerged in the action. The outline he projects at such a moment, the picture of the carefully self-defining, poised hero, is one with which the audience will already be familiar—the exotically dignified Othello, the courteous and philosophical Hamlet, the scornfully provocative Coriolanus. But the outline contains a horde of new stresses that threaten to tear the outlined self apart—and which earlier in the play have done so. When Othello turns to his captors at "Soft you, a word or two before you go," we watch the actor reassume the same style of command over his audience on stage that he exerted in his first-act speech before the Senate—the same quietness of presentation, the orator-general's self-confidence, the deliberate simplicity, even the judicious exoticism, a style that takes pleasure in its honesty and self-control. But into this outline must flow all the irretrievable shame of Othello's situation, what he has done, what he knows his audience thinks of him, what he is about to do. The actor who simply "reverts" to the identity of the earlier Othello—who simply plays the Senate speech again—will fail here; he must make us feel that the new definition of self is earned, that it takes its place in full response to all the confusions of self that have reduced Othello to gibberish, have led him to murder, humiliation, and irretrievable remorse. Othello reachieves his old style in spite of his loss of "occupation" and "content," and this gives the style new dignity and terror.

Similarly, Hamlet's reflective speeches are not simply pauses in the action, glimpses of an earlier, less distraught hero—they are moments when he attempts to integrate his new experience into some kind of poise, some kind of wholeness of being. Too often, both in discussing the content of these speeches and in performing them, we lose sight of either the stresses they should play against or the integration they attempt. The calmer speeches, like the address to the players or his reflections on "the stamp of one defect" while he waits for the Ghost to appear, represent a kind of poise that Hamlet frequently draws upon when he needs to hold himself in readiness, when he is waiting for the "invisible event." His deftness in articulation at these points, the flexibility and humaneness of his discourse, allow us to see him maintaining his composure and his faculties in the face of inner and outer threat. The address to the players, for example, must be the speech of a man on the verge of a great confrontation (the play-within-the-play is moments away), a man moreover fresh from his horrible interview with Ophelia. "Readiness" is an important word in *Hamlet*, and one impression Hamlet strongly projects at various moments in the play is of a man ready for anything. (It is not always a very comforting impression.)

Hamlet's reflective speeches help mark stages in his

development, in which the reflective poise is maintained against increasingly complex stresses, and the reflection grows closer and closer to the heart of Hamlet's mystery. At the end of the play he is not simply a man ready to risk death—we have seen him at that pitch before—but ready *for* death. His speech to Horatio about providence is above all the action of a man who has done and suffered much violence, a man waiting for something terrible to break out, who without any loss of readiness is able both to put his soul in order and exchange gracious discourse with his friend:

> *Not a whit, we defy augury. There is special provi-*
> *dence in the fall of a sparrow. If it be now, tis not to*
> *come; if it be not to come, it will be now; if it be not*
> *now, yet it will come. The readiness is all. Since no man*
> *of aught he leaves knows, what is't to leave betimes?*
> *Let be.*

That "let be" must seem to respond to all Hamlet has struggled with in the play, and strike us not as a retreat but as a movement forward. Shakespeare reinforces the effect by juxtaposing the line with the arrival of Claudius and the court, prepared, as we know, for the duel that has been rigged to kill Hamlet. The advancing crowd is, in effect, a great engine of death, and Hamlet's "let be" rings out as it approaches.

* * *

Hamlet is the most interesting play ever written—and one reason for this is that it is immediately concerned with the nature of theatrical interest itself, with the relation of the actor's art to life. So it is no surprise that it pays special attention to the process of identification on-stage and off, and that it is alert to the connections between the two, to the ways in which the problems of establishing an effective self in dramatic performance illuminate the more general problem of establishing identity in a mortal world. I want to take advantage of this now, and treat the play as a commentary on our appetite for drama, particularly on the meaning and nature of acting as a mode of experience.

To say, as Hamlet does when we first see him, "I have that within which passeth show," is to challenge provocatively the value of drama; it is to say that no performance can adequately express the self. Hamlet suggests that anything that can be performed may be, indeed is likely to be, a mere pretense ("They are actions that a man might play"). The defiance in Hamlet's assertion exposes a doubt as to identity, for to claim that what is within cannot be shown is to doubt that the self can ever be whole in action or utterance. It is to confess to a weight on the self that the self cannot master; Hamlet's belief in the unactability of what is within him is at one with the overwhelming depression he confesses to in his first soliloquy:

> How weary, stale, flat, and unprofitable
> Seem to me all the uses of this world.

The world disgusts him, and all actions in it are meaningless. His position is similar to Cordelia's initial refusal of all show at the beginning of *Lear*. In both plays, these anti-theatrical refusals are preludes to an upheaval and chaos in the visible world we feel reflects an inner upheaval of the self.

In Hamlet's case the upheaval—which causes him to question the very foundations of being and to wish he had never been born—comes about because he is enjoined to *act*. Just as his profound attachment to his father has driven him to find all actions meaningless, it now leads him to devote himself to pursuing his father's instructions to act—and to act as a revenger, which means construct

ing an action of a peculiarly elaborate, meaningful, and .
self-consciously theatrical kind. It is theatrical in many
senses, but perhaps most of all in that, against the
background of a world in which all actions are ambiguous, in which a gesture of love may be a springe to catch a
woodcock, in which it is hard to tell the difference
between a spirit of health and a goblin damned, in which
even to be and not to be are ambiguously intertwined—
against this background, Hamlet as a revenger is called
upon to construct an action whose climax must be an
emblematic punishment, as clear as it is satisfying. It
must not only achieve its immediate end—the death of
Claudius—and do so through disguise and plotting, but it
must be, as the revenge genre requires, a properly
significant killing, vengeance for a foul and unnatural
murder. Its meanings must be made unambiguously
visible to an on-stage audience, in this case the Danish
court.

Hamlet's efforts to accomplish his task lead him, of
course, into the most elaborate disguises and scenarios.
Starting as a man who rejects all activity as play-acting,
he becomes not only an actor—assuming the antic disposition, speaking daggers but using none—but a playwright, and even an instructor of actors. Significantly, the
kind of growth required of him strikingly resembles a
process that may be observed both in the psychic development of children and the training of professional
actors. Psychologists describe this process as the movement from "play-action" to "play-acting," from the immediate expression of emotion in action, to the transformation of emotions into impersonations, "scripted" and
controlled:

> *Play* action *is characterized by the unmodified ex-*
> *pression of the instincts of love and hate in the form of*

> *play. Play acting utilizes a more mature . . . process of mental functioning in which the instinctual expression is subservient to the specific play. . . . Normally, as the child grows, play action gives way to play acting. Stage acting encompasses both activities. However, the actor who is limited to the play-action level of his art is usually an inferior, exhibitionistic artist and may be emotionally disturbed. The play-acting actor controls and regulates his acting technique and therefore is likely to be a competent professional.*

Hamlet makes a similar distinction to the actors:

> *Nor do not saw the air too much with your hand, thus, but use all gently, for in the very torrent, tempest, and (as I may say) whirlwind of your passion, you must acquire and beget a temperance that may give it smoothness.*

Otherwise, as he points out, some necessary question of the play may be neglected. The smoothness and temperance Hamlet requires here are the professional regulation of emotion the play-acting actor has mastered. It is the technique Hamlet himself must master in order to respond successfully to his own cue for action. The play-action of the earlier scenes, the sulky silences and wild outbursts, are gradually left behind when, in response to the Ghost's injunction, he learns he must behave like a trained actor and even a writer of plays.

The unregulated outbursts do not vanish entirely. Hamlet's rage and anguish are always close to the surface and he finds it difficult to control them, but we soon see him struggling to accommodate his painful emotions to play-acting. At the end of the second act, when Hamlet contrasts the Player's feigned passion over Hecuba with his own real emotion, he flies into a fury in which he rants like a conventional stage revenger, but then he suddenly stops and sees his outburst as a kind of performance:

Bloody, bawdy villain!
Remorseless, treacherous, lecherous, kindless villain!
O, vengeance!
Why, what an ass am I! This is most brave,
That I, the son of a dear father murdered,
Prompted to my revenge by heaven and hell,
Must, like a whore, unpack my heart with words
And fall a-cursing like a very drab,
A scullion! Fie upon't, foh!

This shift of focus, which enables him to see his play-action as play-acting, apparently allows him to go a step further, for, now, he realizes that he can use drama itself as part of his plot for revenge:

> . . . Fie upon't, foh! About, my brains.
> Hum—
> I have heard that guilty creatures sitting at a play . . .
> . . . The play's the thing
> Wherein I'll catch the conscience of the King.

In our own lives, too, the transition from play-action to play-acting is never complete, and as with Hamlet or the perpetually struggling actor, it is repeated constantly in the effort to build a coherent and effective self.

The child develops "character" (control over his emotions, power over other people's) as the actor develops the power to play characters. Like the child's, the actor's play-acting grows out of play-action. The leap by which he takes on another identity depends, to begin with, on his capacity for emotional expressiveness, his ability to act out the aggression inside him ("unmodified expression . . . of love and hate"), the play of intense reactions to the external world. But the leap is complete only when he applies some regulation—some governing aggression, we might say—to this instinctive play. Once more we come upon the paradox of acting, and here we may see that it involves a peculiarly ambiguous relation to sincerity. Only when you "modify" your emotions, that is, alter them, can you "play" them successfully. Not surprisingly, sincerity presents a problem Hamlet must struggle with too. When we first see him he is positively tongue-tied with sincerity, oppressed by a sense that all action must falsify what he feels. Polonius puts the problem glibly— the important thing, he says, is to be true to one's self. But for Hamlet sincerity in action is no simple matter. As the play progresses, we encounter a number of characters who are obviously true to themselves, who enjoy a simple relation of inner feeling to outward act. They make the conventional gestures with no sense of ambiguity. But the obvious "sincerity" of Laertes, Fortinbras, and the First Player leaves Hamlet either irritated or envious. Their simple directness or simple artifice—attractive as it may at moments seem—is not adequate to his difficulty, any more than it would be to an actor who wanted to play Hamlet's part.

Hamlet's development is a paradigm of the problem of sincerity in its radical form, the form which connects the problem of sincerity with our appetite for drama. What Hamlet, children, and actors have in common is that they are haunted—and compelled by what haunts them to "act." Feeling incomplete, robbed, or betrayed, they are driven by some ghostly, elusive force—almost against their will—from play-action to play-acting; they must make up for the grief that passes show with a series of passionately maintained disguises. Surely they experience, in aggravated form, a struggle within the self that goes on ceaselessly in each of us, that drives us all to some kind of concocted selfhood, thrown together to meet the slings and arrows of daily life, and leaves always some residue of longing for a clearer self, for fuller freedom, for sharply defined and true identity. I said earlier that the self discovers its identity in fear and deprivation. It is through our relationship with the ghosts who arise at that discovery—with unstable, inexorable, haunting presences disturbingly like our parents, as disturbing in their sorrow as in their anger, arousing fear and urgency and guilt—that we begin to learn, like Hamlet, about the dangerous forces lying within us and around us. What these ghosts are, psychology still struggles to learn. They are, perhaps, instinctive or acquired fears, innate aggressions, scars left by various traumas— the shocks that flesh is heir to—suppressed desires, memories of our parents, patterns and relations we are doomed to repeat (or, as we say, to "re-enact"). They may be some or all of these, or perhaps something entirely different. For our purposes, it is only necessary to acknowledge that, whatever they are, they haunt us, and begin to haunt us as we begin to discover that we are separate, beleaguered selves. It is our ghosts who force us to take action and to make the pretenses, true or false, that taking action requires. It is our ghosts—all the hauntedness we carry around inside us—who make it hard for us, impossible really, to be true to ourselves, to that within which passes show. For no matter what it does, the self cannot achieve the identification it desires in real life, it can only approximate it, and usually at the kind of cost that tragedy suggests. The theatricality of daily life, however necessary, is always at least partially a withdrawal, a compromise, a falsification, a way of covering up. In the theater, however, it can become a way of opening out, without that sense of compromise. This is not to deprecate real life in order to make a case for theater, nor to deny that it is through the great leaps of role playing and play-acting, through imperfect masks and partial truths, that we must blossom into action in our lives, if blossom we can. It is merely to note that the special awareness of a complete identification in the present, which our daily play-acting both points toward and recognizes as impossible, does become available to us in the theater when we respond to and participate in the actor's art. Our ghosts make play-actors of us all, but they also attract us to actors and the theater. We turn to drama as the Tangkul and Orokolo did, to drive our ghosts away. Even the blandest commercial play does this, though in the most obvious, least satisfying fashion —for example, an old baddy is defeated, and his money and his daughter are given to some nicely cosmeticized version of ourselves. What more could we want? Only when we get more do we know. In better hands, we find that ghosts can be expelled from regions much closer to our hearts—closer to the wounds where our identities began. What all drama, of whatever quality, works to drive away are the ghosts that keep us blurred and incomplete, longing for and frightened by completion.

But this is only half the story. For the aim of drama, as we have seen, is not simply to expel ghosts but to win their power for the living, to invest the self with the power of what frightens it, keeps it incomplete, hunts it down. One could say that, in the theater, we join the actors in repeating that step into selfhood-through-play-acting which we first made as children. Only now we can step, as we could not then and cannot elsewhere, into a free and full identity. The tragic process makes it possible for Hamlet, in the teeth of everything, to be true to himself in the audience's mind, to have an actor-like definiteness that seems nevertheless to be in contact with the most painful confusions and uncertainties of our existence. He achieves a complete unfolding—as drama generally makes it possible for actors-as-characters to achieve some kind of unique truth-to-self in which the audience participates. Truth-to-self, hauntingness, identification, freedom—I have used all these terms, at different times, to suggest the kind of strangeness-in-action that affects us in the theater, and I have also suggested that they may be used as touchstones in the analysis of individual plays or the drama of particular eras. The words are so interrelated as at times to be nearly interchangeable, for they all serve to express the powerful yet elusive claim which the processes of acting exercise upon us. I have said that Hamlet haunts Elsinore as the Ghost has haunted him; it is the power of ghosts to act and be free that actors take on in performance, and that we ourselves take on, watching them perform.

* * *

It seems a given quality of human consciousness to imagine a clarity of self of which the self is incapable, and to judge, guide, criticize the self, indeed to lead one's life, in terms of achieving this ideal clarity. In *Hamlet* all the fundamental conditions of pain, loss, and failure that define the self against its will and make impossible the triumphant self-definition for which the self is destined to long—all these conditions are heightened and pressed forward on the audience's consciousness. They are familiar to the psyche from infancy: the labyrinth of our attachment to parents; the horror of death; our fear of darkness, poison, cold, and the unknown; the sense of indefinable corruption at work in everything; the sinister ambiguity of all gestures. Against this we watch the career of Prince Hamlet, learning the need for theater in his life—playing role upon role, adopting disguise within disguise—in order to be true to himself. These are all "actions that a man might play," but they are the only actions available, and life needs this giving and hazarding, this thrust toward self-definition in action.

To possess genuine identity, to achieve a free and unbewildered clarity of being, to define oneself through action in the world though every action threatens to compromise the self because it exposes the self as fundamentally unclear and incomplete—this is the continuing project of the self, in one sense necessary, in another impossible. It is also the project, as Hamlet discovers, that only theater accomplishes, and for this reason, identification, as I have been calling it, stands at the center of the uniqueness of dramatic art, and bears decisively upon the human needs drama satisfies, the kind of meaning it makes, the special relation it establishes between ourselves and the world.

*   *   *

One reason Shakespeare has kept his appeal for the modern audience is his very modern sense of the fragility of identity. His heroes do not simply press forward to express themselves through mastery or self-annihilation in the Elizabethan fashion; they often waver and search, looking for a lost or fragmented identity, as Hamlet does. Much modern drama—and especially American drama—takes its shape from this awareness of identity as compromised not simply by the pressure of otherness but by the problematic epistemology of selfhood. Very often the modern dramatic hero, consciously or not, is working to gather up the fragments of an elusive conception of self, trying to "find out who he is." And in this task he is usually stymied by conflicting signals. As he tries to act out one kind of identification, he betrays another.

Willy Loman, for example, is one of a number of American dramatic heroes whose identification consists in an effort to possess his memories. These memories are dramatic because haunting, because they press forward on Willy and his sons with a burden of conflicting self-definitions, definitions of "success" which are both deeply personal to Willy, radiating from the various fatherly figures he intimately admires, and at the same time crushingly external to him. Is it the Whitmanesque American sagehood of his own father, the capitalist glamour of Dave Singleman, or the ruthless cunning of brother Ben that speaks to him of his true being? Is it the roar of the crowd, the law of the jungle, or the freedom of the frontier that best expresses the life of a salesman? "The man didn't know who he was," says Biff at the end, one voice in a choral epilogue after Willy's suicide, in which each voice has only a partial truth.

The effort to possess one's past is perhaps a natural American theme, and it takes the form, in the greatest American plays, of an attempt to possess one's family—to move among the memories or among the actual events of a childhood trying to sort out the disguises and deceptions, to define one's parents or oneself. It is O'Neill's recurrent theme (reaching its most personal and perfected form in *Long Day's Journey into Night*) and it is Tennessee Williams'. Tom, in *The Glass Menagerie*, tries to master his past by becoming its narrator. He is trying to define himself by breaking out of the trapped, deluded world of his mother's apartment with its crippling memories and graces. All his efforts are bound up with the drive toward narration, whether it be in his attacks on his mother, in which he tries to translate his resentment into a fictional portrait of himself as a rebel ("I run a string of cathouses in the Valley, mother!"), or in his actual attempts to become a writer, or in his main activity in the play—his effort to narrate, to speak to us, to transform the play's action into his own action of self-expression. But Tom also cannot put together a complete self. What he possesses at the end are fragments; and their contradictions sadden him even as they define him. Though free and on his own, he is still part of the glass menagerie; no wonder he remains haunted (and this quality must control his whole performance) by the menagerie's possessor, by the sad, puzzling, lost presence of his sister.

American dramatists have tended to locate the awareness of lost or contradictory identity in the contradictions of American society and the American family, but the theme is not only American. It stems from the larger epistemological crisis of our era, in which the self is seen to be lost among its means of knowledge, indeed in which our methods for knowing the world and articulating the self finally cut us off from both world and self. Peter Handke in his remarkable *Kaspar* succeeds in reducing the crisis to its basic and most extreme epistemological terms. Here, the human capacity for speech is presented both as our only means to selfhood and as a trap from which we cannot escape. Handke's hero, starting out in a kind of pre-linguistic infancy, discovers, as we all do, that he can identify himself through sentences. But sentences take away your identity. Without the structures of language, you cannot express yourself, but once you possess them you can express only what the structures allow. The language shapes your experience and makes you conform to society's notion of what a self can be. You cannot become a person without speech, but speech lets you say only what others can say. "I want to be somebody . . ." begins the sentence the inarticulate Kaspar hears as he stumbles about at the play's beginning. It is the model sentence, by which he will learn the power of sentences, learn to control his body and his mind, learn, in short, to be somebody, to have an identity. But the whole sentence, dinned into his ears while he staggers and struggles, is, "I want to be somebody, like somebody else was once."

*   *   *

Art, in Nietzsche's phrase, is a metaphysical supplement to life, and what I have been exploring in this book is the particular addition to life that drama makes. I said at the

beginning that drama was a means by which man at-
tempted to complete his relation to the world, and I think
that the meaning of that phrase may be clearer by now.
These chapters have, I hope, suggested that there is a way
of possessing the world and ourselves that drama provides, which our other experience of life both pressingly
recommends to us and absolutely forbids. The plays we
have just been considering all explore with a very modern
self-consciousness and self-doubt the age-old problem of
finding and constituting an identity. But this problem and
the excitements it breeds have always been very close to
the sources of drama—and drama speaks to the problem
in unique fashion. If it is possible to trace an age's notions
and doubts about identity through the kinds of identification it allows its actors to make, this is because acting,
and hence drama itself, draws its vital appeal from the
paradoxical and painful way in which the idea of our own
identity takes shape in our perceptions.

The importance of identification in drama is bound up
with drama's immediacy. What makes the actor's mimesis different from that of other artists, what makes his
process touch so intimately upon the elementary material
of our fears and our awareness of self, is that he works
with his whole body. He gives us, to live with, not the
product of his body but the body itself. It is in the theater,
we could say, that the body comes in closest contact with
the possibilities of the mind. There we find a present
beyond the limitations of the present, a selfhood beyond
the limits of self. And we find this selfhood not in
symbols, not in memory, and not alone, but in the flesh, in
society, here and now. The special charge of significance
that space and time take on in the theater is a natural
extension and accompaniment of the special definition
that the self exhibits and acquires there. We identify with
actors because the self longs for clarification, because it

longs to possess the present, and possess itself in the present, in a way that ordinary space, time, and selfhood do not allow. Theater exists because our being needs it or is incomplete without it. It seems to me that everywhere about us in our lives we sense a stirring and disturbing potential—a potential for just this kind of definition, for clarification and completeness in the flesh, in the present. This is one of the reasons, for example, that we like to play roles in ordinary life; they provide us with something of this charged sense of significance and definition—the sense, for instance, that a ground exists for our acts, both in the world and in us, the sense that our acts hold together to form an action. But even in role playing, we feel this definition at best as something potential, something, as Tamburlaine says, that "wills us to wear ourselves and never rest," that fills life with hope and longing and restlessness and frustration. There can be no formula, finally, to sum up the appeal of drama. But perhaps I can best leave my subject (and leave it, as I hope, to others who will take it further) by saying: Of this stirring and disturbing potential, drama is the actual.

REFERENCE NOTES

* * *

Part One: Actor and Audience

Page

5–6. "Aristotle acknowledges that . . ." *Poetics* 1447a and 1448a. It is just possible that, in the first of these passages, Aristotle makes a glancing claim for the significance of the actor's art. See Gerald Else, *Aristotle's Poetics: The Argument* (Cambridge, Mass., 1963), pp. 20–22. If so, however, he scarcely elaborates. Indeed, it is uncertain whether Aristotle is even referring to acting here. If the actor does make an appearance in these passages, he is invoked, at best, through disembodied references to "voice," "speech," and "dialogue" that, in effect, either assimilate his contribution to the poet's representation of an event, or split it up into constituent media, like sound and gesture, which the actor—like a musician or sculptor—may be thought to manipulate. Later (1449b), Aristotle refers to acting, in passing, as an aspect of "spectacle," a subject he considers of distinctly secondary importance in dramatic theory. Throughout the *Poetics*, he tends to see the action of drama not as something the actors do, but as what the people in the story do. For the implications of this approach and its influence on contemporary theory, see my discussion, pp. 29–33.

For a full analysis of the complexities of the passages referred to, see Else, *op. cit.*, and Leon Golden and O. B. Hardison, Jr.,

Page

   Aristotle's Poetics: A Translation and Commentary for Students of Literature (Englewood Cliffs, N.J., 1968).

8. "Iona and Peter Opie . . ." *Children's Games in Street and Playground* (Oxford, 1969).

8. "mass hysteria . . . impersonation . . ." See E. R. Dodds's introduction to his edition of Euripides' *Bacchae* (Oxford, 1960), pp. xvii ff. For maenadism, see Dodds's appendix on the subject in *The Greeks and the Irrational* (Boston, 1957), pp. 270–282.

8. "The shaman . . . impersonates . . ." This is not the place to attempt a survey of the literature of shamanism, but two particularly useful books for the student of drama may be mentioned. These are Mircea Eliade, *Shamanism: Archaic Techniques of Ecstasy* (Princeton, 1964) and Andreas Lommel, *The World of the Early Hunters* (London, 1967). For a more sociological approach to the significance of shamanism, see I. M. Lewis, *Ecstatic Religion* (Harmondsworth, Eng., 1971).

8. "Impersonation of the dead . . ." A particularly interesting survey of this phenomenon is still to be found in Sir William Ridgeway, *The Dramas and Dramatic Dances of Non-European Races in Special Reference to the Origin of Greek Tragedy* (Cambridge, 1915).

9. " 'ontological subversiveness.' " Jonas Barish, "The Antitheatrical Prejudice," *Critical Quarterly*, VIII, 4 (Winter, 1966), 331. Along with the same writer's "Exhibitionism and the Antitheatrical Prejudice," *ELH*, XXXVI, 1 (March, 1969), this essay provides an extremely illuminating discussion of the varying and sometimes competing philosophical conceptions of the significance of acting from Plato to the present day.

9. "not to be interfered with." As Stanley Cavell has pointed out in a brilliant study of the phenomenology of performance, there is a sense in which the actor (or, as I would say, the actor-as-character) *cannot* be interfered with. To succeed in doing so—to leap up from your seat and prevent Othello from strangling Desdemona, for instance—is not to affect the character but to stop the performance. When that happens, the actor-as-character simply ceases to exist. See Part Two of Cavell's "The Avoidance of Love: A Reading of *King Lear*," in *Must We Mean What We Say?* (New York, 1969), especially pp. 327–30.

9. "Freud . . . essay on the uncanny . . ." First published in 1919, "The 'Uncanny' " is conveniently available in Volume IV of the *Collected Papers* (New York, 1959).

9. " 'He told . . . see before.' " *Adventures of Huckleberry Finn* (Boston, 1958), p. 115 (Chapter XXI).

Page

10. "A . . . portrait of Garrick." Benjamin Wilson's portrait is best appreciated when compared with G. C. Lichtenberg's eyewitness description of Garrick in the Ghost scene. Both may be found in Kalman A. Burnim, *David Garrick, Director* (Pittsburgh, 1961), pp. 96–97, 159–60.

12. "Arctic hysteria." Here is an account of one form of this disorder:

> Amürakh *is a malady in which the sufferer is frightened . and has a tendency to imitate everything he sees taking place around him. He shows a special proclivity for indulging in obscenities. . . . "The attack . . . is generally manifested in a groundless, instantaneous imitation of another person. A sudden shout uttered by another person is enough to make the sufferer shudder with terror and repeat his model's every movement, no matter how wanton."*

From Lommel, *World of the Early Hunters*, p. 38. (Quoting from M. A. Czaplicka, *Aboriginal Siberia*.)

13. "maenadism." See note to page 8 above.

13. "to worship Dionysus is to begin to act." See Margarete Bieber, *The History of the Greek and Roman Theater* (Princeton, 1961), pp. 1–2. We must be careful not to assume, simply because a clear affinity exists between Dionysiac religion and dramatic performance, that drama in Greece—or elsewhere—actually originated in Dionysiac celebrations. For a stimulating critique of the evidence for the Dionysiac origin of Greek tragedy, see Gerald Else, *The Origin and Early Form of Greek Tragedy* (Cambridge, Mass., 1965), Chapter I.

14. " 'the principle . . . to assimilate.' " Dodds, ed. *Bacchae*, p. xx.

16. " 'a center . . . of busybodies . . .' " Introduction to *Naked Masks: Five Plays by Luigi Pirandello* (New York, 1952), xviii.

16. "John Holloway . . ." *The Story of the Night* (London, 1961).

17. "Norman Rabkin." *Shakespeare and the Common Understanding* (New York, 1967).

18. "hamartia . . ." See *Poetics*, 1453a.

20. " 'ritual forms' . . . the Cambridge anthropologists . . ." The first analysis of Greek tragedy in terms of the patterns of fertility ritual is Gilbert Murray's "Excursus on the Ritual Forms Preserved in Greek Tragedy," in Jane Harrison's *Themis* (Cambridge, 1912). Two years later Francis Cornford applied the theory to comedy in *The Origin of Attic Comedy* (Cambridge, 1914). Cornford's introduction includes a useful, if brief, summary of the tragic pattern according to Murray. Murray, Harrison, and Cornford all drew heavily, of course, on Sir James Frazer's *The Golden Bough*. It should perhaps be noted that Murray was an Oxford man.

Page
25. "Egyptian Coronation Play." This unique work, dating back perhaps as far as 3300 B.C., was discovered in 1896, and first interpreted and translated (into German) by Kurt Sethe in 1928. An English version may be found in Theodore Gaster, *Thespis* (New York, 1950), pp. 376–99. Information about the ceremony is far too fragmentary to pronounce on with any confidence, but my guess is that the coronation "play" is no more a genuine drama than the Mass. As the Catholic priest represents Christ by virtue of his office, so, in the coronation ceremony, the new Egyptian king represented the god Horus. Though it is unquestionably a beautiful and sophisticated work, full of powerful spectacle and remarkable juxtapositions of visual and verbal imagery, I see no evidence of anything that could be called histrionic energy. Even what Gaster translates as a "ritual punching match" seems entirely ceremonial and symbolic. There is nothing in it comparable to the Angel's calling the Marys back.

25. "drama in the medieval church." See O. B. Hardison, Jr.'s immensely illuminating *Christian Rite and Christian Drama in the Middle Ages* (Baltimore, 1965), especially Chapters II and V. For evidence of histrionic elements in the Mass, see pp. 78–79. Professor Hardison, I should add, sees more enactment in the medieval Mass than I do, and entertains a broader and (I would say) more "literary" notion of drama. Still, one cannot quarrel with his account of medieval drama in terms that connect its meaning and significance to the meaning and significance of the Mass. The connection is real, and Hardison's analysis is an exemplary fusion of exact scholarship and sensitive criticism.

26. "The Kaingang of Brazil . . ." René Girard, *La Violence et le Sacré* (Paris, 1972), p. 82, citing Jules Henry, *Jungle People* (New York, 1964).

27. "malevolent chaotic externality." See Mircea Eliade, *The Sacred and the Profane* (New York, 1959), p. 29.

27. "T. S. Eliot . . ." *Selected Essays*, 3d ed. (London, 1951), p. 52.

29. " 'We conventionally . . . the hevehe.' " Schechner, "Actuals: Primitive Ritual and Performance Theory," *Theatre Quarterly* (London), I, 2 (April–June, 1971), 58–59. *Fluids* is a happening by Allan Kaprow. The Tiwi Trial is a highly ritualized form of trial by combat, described in Charles Hart and Arnold Pilling, *The Tiwi of North Australia* (New York, 1966). The dancing of the hevehe is part of a remarkable dramatic cycle lasting several years, performed by the Orokolo of New Guinea, and described in an equally remarkable book by the anthropologist, F. E. Williams, *Drama of Orokolo* (Oxford, 1940).

Page
31–32. " 'The goal . . . the performer.' " Schechner, *loc. cit.*, 58.
34–35. "Eliot as a young man . . ." See "Four Elizabethan Dramatists," in *Selected Essays*, 3d ed., p. 111. Checking the dates, I see that Eliot was thirty-five at the time the essay appeared. Whether this is young, I am not prepared to argue; Eliot's remarks significantly antedate his practical experience of the theater—and sound like it.
36. " 'This stage . . . of stage-movers.' " F. E. Williams, *Orokaiva Society* (London, 1930), p. 240.
36. "Beyond the Pleasure Principle . . ." The references may be found in the Bantam Matrix edition (New York, 1967), pp. 32–34.
36. "Erik Erikson . . ." *Childhood and Society*, 2d ed. (New York, 1963), pp. 215–18.
36. "R. D. Laing . . ." *The Divided Self* (Baltimore, 1963), p. 118.
38. "our aggression toward them." See Freud, *Totem and Taboo* (London, 1950), pp. 59–63.
38. "among the Tangkul . . ." See Ridgeway, *Dramas and Dramatic Dances* . . . , pp. 211–15. Ridgeway is drawing on T. C. Hodson's *The Nagas of Manipur*. Whether the ceremony is still performed I do not know.
39. " 'At that . . . evil spirit.' " Knud Rasmussen, *The Intellectual Culture of the Copper Eskimos* (Copenhagen, 1932), p. 58.
39. " 'All feel . . . he sees.' " *Ibid.*, p. 60.
39–40. " 'We saw . . . the blizzard.' " *Ibid.*, p. 61.
40. "a scene that looks like . . ." *Othello*, III, iii.
40. "Timon . . . drives Apemantus away . . ." *Timon of Athens*, IV, iii.
41. "the *samuna*." My account is taken from F. E. Williams, *Orokaiva Society*, pp. 244 ff.
42. " 'I have . . . some importance.' " *Ibid.*, p. 251.
42. " 'Altogether his . . . audience laugh.' " *Ibid.*
43. "Gilbert Murray . . ." *Hamlet and Orestes* (New York, 1914).
44. "of Elizabethan drama . . ." The best study of the connections between the Vice and his dramatic descendants is Bernard Spivack, *Shakespeare and the Allegory of Evil* (New York, 1958).
45. "compromise the professed piety . . ." Cf. Muriel Bradbrook, *The Rise of the Common Player* (Cambridge, Mass., 1962), p. 129.
46. "Garrick . . . impressed Diderot . . ." *The Paradox of Acting* (New York, 1957), pp. 32–33.
46. " 'Didst thou . . . not thyself?' " *Ibid.*, p. 46.
47. "Use of human skins . . ." See E. O. James, *Origins of Sacrifice* (London, 1937), pp. 85–90.

Page
47. " 'A mask . . . of death.' " Jean-Louis Barrault, *The Theatre of Jean-Louis Barrault* (New York, 1961), pp. 76–77.
48. " 'A, at . . . the experimenter.' " C. W. Valentine, *The Normal Child and Some of His Abnormalities* (Baltimore, 1956), p. 127.
48. " 'The child . . . the doll.' " Donald Kaplan, "Theatre Architecture: A Derivation of the Primal Cavity," *The Drama Review*, XII, 3 (Spring, 1968), 110. He is describing an experiment filmed by Renè Spitz.
49. "omnipotence of thoughts." See "The 'Uncanny,' " *Collected Papers*, IV, 393 ff.
49. " 'primal dialogue.' " Spitz's use of the term and its relevance to the interaction of actors and audiences are discussed by Kaplan in the article cited above, pp. 109 ff.
49–50. "Muriel Bradbrook . . ." *English Dramatic Form* (London, 1965). See pp. 47–51 for her discussion of *Tamburlaine*.

Part Two: Hero and Play

Page
56. " a quasi-religious dignitary . . ." The celebrity of the Greek actor increased enormously in the fourth century, and most of our evidence as to his status is drawn from that period and later; but there is no doubt that even in the fifth century, the actor enjoyed an esteem rare in the history of Western theater, and was considered a religious minister by virtue of his role in the festival of Dionysus. See Bieber, *The History of the Greek and Roman Theater*, p. 83.
57. " 'Wonders are . . . than man.' " *Antigone*, 332.
57. "Bernard Knox's . . . *Oedipus at Thebes* . . ." (New Haven, 1957).
58. "C. L. Barber . . ." *Shakespeare's Festive Comedy* (Princeton, 1959), p. 193.
60. "her great dialogue . . ." *Phèdre*, II, v.
66. " 'modern Niobe-tragedy'. . ." See Martin Esslin, *Brecht* (New York, 1961), p. 230.
67. "Dionysiac lightness . . ." Dionysus appears in Shaw's work as the life force to which his leading characters unite themselves, as, for example, Jack Tanner does when he marries Ann Whitefield in *Man and Superman*. A superb Shavian image of this "marriage in Dionysus" occurs at the end of *Androcles and the Lion*, when hero

Page

and lion dance together in the arena, before the astonished Roman audience. The mixture of comic gaiety and union with a superhuman power is profoundly characteristic of Shaw's art. Dionysus is explicitly and repeatedly invoked, with full sensitivity to his dramatic and religious significance, in *Major Barbara*, a play dedicated to Gilbert Murray, which includes an extended quotation from Murray's recent translation of the *Bacchae*, and features Murray himself in the character of Adolphus Cusins, the professor of Greek who inherits a munitions empire. The play may profitably be interpreted as Shaw's version of the *Bacchae*.

69. "Weiss . . . pronouncements since . . ." See Eric Bentley, "Peter Weiss and Wolf Biermann," *The Nation*, Jan. 10, 1966.

72. "Stanislavsky . . . missed the point . . ." See David Magarshack, *Chekhov: A Life* (New York, 1953), pp. 379–80.

78. "sit in God's throne." See R. W. Hanning, " 'You Have Begun a Parlous Pleye': The Nature and Limits of Dramatic Mimesis as a Theme in Four Middle English 'Fall of Lucifer' Cycle Plays," *Comparative Drama*, VII, 1 (Spring, 1973), 22–50.

78. *"The Play Called Corpus Christi . . ."* (Stanford, 1966). For the idea of drama as play see especially pp. 8–32.

79. "the identity of their victim." Kolve, pp. 174–99.

82. " '*Deliberate illusion* . . . ordinary reality.' " Jean Piaget, *Play, Dreams and Imitation in Childhood* (New York, 1962), p. 168.

83. " 'does not . . . they are.' " *Ibid.*

83. "The play protects the ego-universe." Among the attributes of play, Huizinga lists rules, orderly procedure, secrecy, and disguise. See *Homo Ludens* (London, 1949), p. 13. The effect of such devices, of course, is to insulate the activity—not simply to stress the special nature of play but to give it a protective structure. And it is exactly in its use of these protective devices that drama most resembles play; in that, and in the general sense of elated, absorbed freedom it induces.

84. "Donald Kaplan . . ." "Gestures, Sensibilities, Scripts: Further Reflections on Performance/Audience Interaction," *Performance*, 1 (December, 1971), 31–46.

84. " 'The script . . . not made.' " *Ibid.*, 37.

87. " 'adaptive' . . . 'assimilative.' " See *Play, Dreams and Imitation in Childhood*, passim.

88. " 'At 3:11 . . . dead duck.' " *Ibid.*, p. 133.

89. "Writing about Falstaff . . ." *Shakespeare and the Energies of Drama* (Princeton, 1972), p. 56.

91. "Arnold . . ." "On the Modern Element in Literature," *The Complete Works of Matthew Arnold*, ed. R. H. Super (Ann Arbor, 1960), I, 18–37.

Page
94. "shocked Athenian audience . . ." See Sir Arthur Pickard-Cambridge, *The Dramatic Festivals of Athens*, 2d ed. (Oxford, 1968), pp. 264–65.

95. "1588 . . ." The date is not exact, but must be very close. Neither *Tamburlaine* nor the *Spanish Tragedy* can be put much before 1587 or much after 1589. It is always possible, of course, that a lost earlier play of their type and caliber may one day come to light, but after several decades of diligent search, it seems unlikely.

96. "the stage-world was consistent and complete." Cf. Muriel Bradbrook, *The Rise of the Common Player* (Cambridge, Mass., 1962), p. 128.

98. "To argue that Kyd . . . is more indebted to Virgil . . ." For an influential critique of the Senecan contribution to English tragedy along these lines, see Howard Baker, *Induction to Tragedy* (Baton Rouge, 1939).

100. "Machiavellian *virtù.*" See Irving Ribner, "The Idea of History in *Tamburlaine*," *ELH*, XX (1954), 257–58; also Harry Levin, *The Overreacher* (Cambridge, Mass., 1952), pp. 25–27, 179–83.

102. "'When they . . . the fireplace.'" "Discoveries," *The Cutting of an Agate*, now included in *Essays and Introductions* (New York, 1961), p. 274.

103. "such actors' groups." As the comments of their founders attest. See, e.g., Joseph Chaikin, *The Presence of the Actor* (New York, 1972) or Jerzy Grotowski, *Towards a Poor Theater* (New York, 1970).

Part Three: Theater and World

Page
113. " 'Theory' and 'theater' . . ." The semantic connection is offered, of course, by way of illustration and metaphor, and not as proof. That both words derive ultimately from *theasthai* signifies little in itself. But the basic meaning of *theorein* was "to be a spectator," and a range of cognate words could be applied to attendance at public spectacles, including dramatic performances. *Theoroi* were the city's representatives at the festivals of other states. The word could also mean "ambassadors" or "spectators" in general. One must be careful not to draw hasty conclusions from any of these usages, because the notion of "theory" in our sense of the word only develops slowly out of the more general notion of observing

Page

with a lively interest. Serious foreign travel—going abroad to see the world—was called *theoria.*

114. "Quasimodo . . ." *Selected Writings,* trans. Allen Mandelbaum (New York, 1961), p. 11.

114. "William Empson . . ." *Some Versions of Pastoral* (London, 1950).

116. "an unreachable past." Cf. Stanley Cavell, *A World Viewed: Reflections on the Ontology of Film* (New York, 1971), p. 155.

121. "the need to acknowledge . . ." Cf. Cavell, *Must We Mean What We Say?,* (New York, 1969), pp. 330 ff. Cavell goes on, very beautifully, to explore the kinds of acknowledgment that *are* available to an audience. I am simply concerned with the fact that certain demands—call them moral or psychological—which the people we encounter inevitably make on us in ordinary life, vanish in the theater. And this in spite of our being intensely, even passionately, interested in the people we see on stage.

121. "Desdemona from Othello . . ." Cavell's example. See my note to p. 9 above.

122. " 'imperfect self-definition' . . . 'defective body-image' . . ." See Philip Weissman, *Creativity in the Theatre: A Psychoanalytic Study* (New York, 1965), pp. 11–13.

125. "Sophocles makes clear . . ." See Knox, *Oedipus at Thebes,* Chapter I.

130. "transvestism . . . initiation ceremonies . . ." For the significance of transvestism in initiation ritual, see Bruno Bettelheim, *Symbolic Wounds* (New York, 1962).

130–31. " 'Farewell till . . . lose myself.' " *Comedy of Errors,* I, ii, 30–40. Unless otherwise noted, my citations from Shakespeare follow the New Cambridge Edition, ed. W. A. Neilson and C. J. Hill (Boston, 1942).

131. " 'O, rejoice . . . his own.' " *The Tempest,* V, i, 206–13.

134. "Garga outdoes Shlink . . ." *In the Jungle of Cities.*

134. "Shen Te disguises herself . . ." *The Good Woman of Setzuan.*

134. "Brecht's . . . writings on the theater . . ." Brecht's "theory" consists of a vast number of utterances widely varying in type and tone, spanning nearly forty years of theatrical activity, and in most cases directed to highly specific occasions—production notes, interviews, polemics, and the like. A convenient place to study his ideas in their complexity and variousness is John Willett's collection, *Brecht on Theatre* (New York, 1964).

138. "Artaud." See *The Theater and Its Double* (New York, 1958).

139–40. " 'Imagine . . . the outside world.' " Trans. Geoffrey Skelton (New York, 1965), pp. 91–92.

Page
140–41. "DUPERRET *approaches . . . forefinger threateningly."* Ibid., p. 7.

142. "once-fashionable notion . . ." See Sir Sidney Lee, *Shakespeare and the Modern Stage* (London, 1906), p. 42.

142. "Granville-Barker . . ." *Prefaces to Shakespeare* (Princeton, 1946), I, 435–37.

142. "Michael Jamieson . . ." "Shakespeare's Celibate Stage," in *The Seventeenth Century Stage,* ed. G. E. Bentley (Chicago, 1968), pp. 78–91.

143. " 'The quick . . . a whore.' " *Antony and Cleopatra,* V, ii, 216–21.

143. " 'Ah, dear . . . for prey!' " III, xiii, 158–67.

144. " 'Let Rome . . . empire fall!' " I, i, 33–34.

144. " 'Give me . . . is desired.' " V, ii, 283–99.

145. " 'Go fetch . . . Mark Antony.' " Ibid., 227–29.

147. " 'Occupation' and 'content' . . ." See *Othello,* II, i, 185–98.

148. " 'Not a . . . Let be.' " V, ii, 220–25. For *Hamlet,* I follow Edward Hubler's text in his Signet edition (New York, 1963).

150–51. " 'Play action . . . competent professional.' " Weissman, *Creativity in the Theater,* p. 17.

151. " 'Nor do . . . it smoothness.' " III, ii, 4–8.

152. " 'Bloody, bawdy . . . upon't, foh!' " II, ii, 591–99, reading "scullion" with the Folio at 599.

152. " 'Fie upon't . . . the King.' " Ibid., 599–617.

INDEX

* * *

Plays are indexed both as they are named and as they are alluded to by names of characters in the text. Authors are indexed only as their names occur in the text.

* * *